I0004986

INFOBODY
THEORY
AND
INFOBODY
MODEL

YUHU CHE

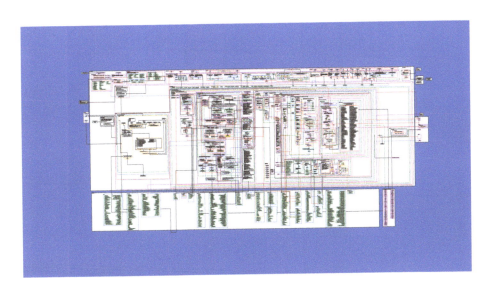

Copyright © 2021 Yuhu Che
All rights reserved
First Edition

PAGE PUBLISHING
Conneaut Lake, PA

First originally published by Page Publishing 2021

ISBN 978-1-6624-5074-7 (pbk)
ISBN 978-1-6624-5075-4 (digital)

Printed in the United States of America

CONTENTS

CHAPTER 1

INFOBODY OVERVIEW

IN NOWADAYS, PEOPLE are talking about information everywhere, such as information science, information technology, information explosion, etc. But what is information? Nobody can simply answer.

If we search online for the definition of information, we will get a variety of definitions. Merriam-Webster listed many aspects of information such as "knowledge obtained from investigation, study, or instruction," "a signal or character (as in a communication system or computer) representing data," etc.

Even in information theory presented by Shannon and other researchers, there is no exact definition for information, and the major topic is about information entropy defined as a probability.

If we think in detail about each piece of information we get, we can see we are actually talking about a text message, a speech, a picture, a video, etc., which are all physical bodies that "contain" some "information." This yields a new concept—infobody.

This book presents this new concept—infobody, which may help us to understand what information is.

1.1 Concept of Infobody

Any physical body that contains information is called an *infobody*. Containing information means it tells people something.

For example, when we say "three," this sound is an infobody. When we write "3" on a piece of paper, this symbol is an infobody. The sound "three" and the symbol "3" contain the same information but in different physical bodies (sound and paper).

In fact, any language is a big set of infobodies. Also, any text is another big set of infobodies. Besides languages and text, any physical body can be an infobody. A flashing left light of a car is an infobody telling people the car is going to turn left. A light in a room is an infobody that tells you someone may be in the room.

Please note any physical body becomes an infobody when and only when at least one person sees it or hears it or smells it or tastes it or feels it by his/her sense organs such as eyes, ears, nose, tongue, and skin. This means when we talk about an infobody, at least one person must be involved. A tree in a virgin forest is not an infobody if nobody sees it. A grain of sand in a desert is not an infobody if nobody sees it.

Any physical body itself is also an infobody that tells people it exists in reality. This kind of infobody is called *reality infobody*. Some infobody not only tells people it exists in reality but also tells something else is called *translative infobody.*

An oral language is a typical translative infobody that translates reality infobodies into sounds. A written text is another typical translative infobody that translates reality infobodies into symbols. The translation between different languages is based on the same reality infobodies. Pictures, videos, and data are all translative infobodies.

Please note, any translative infobody is also a reality infobody. For example, a book is a reality infobody because it exists in reality. It is also a translative infobody because it is telling a story. That story is not a reality infobody.

The infobody concept discussed in this book is to human beings only. We do not discuss any infobodies to dogs or birds.

Reality infobodies mean everything in reality, including the existence and movement of reality infobodies, time, space, energy, etc.

Any infobody must be perceived by one or more people through sensory organs such as eyes, ears, nose, tongue, and skin. For example, when you type some text on your computer, that text is an infobody to you. But the memory holds the text is not an infobody to you because you cannot perceive it at all.

Everything in the brain of a human being is also an infobody. Brain cells are infobodies, and the physical status of brain cells is also infobodies. When you see some reality infobody, your brain creates an image in your brain about that reality infobody. This image is also an infobody, and it is a translative infobody that translates the reality infobody to the image in your brain.

The source of a brain image is called *imagined infobody*. In most cases, the imagined infobody is a reality infobody, but sometimes, an imagined infobody can be a text or any other translative infobody. For example, a novel is telling a story that can generate a lot of images in your brain. That novel is an imagined infobody. Sometimes, an imagined infobody may be hidden, but you can still imagine it. For example, you wrote a letter which is an infobody. When you enclose it in an envelope, you cannot see the letter anymore. When you drop it into a mailbox, it is hidden in that mailbox, but you can still imagine it in your brain.

The "information" in our live language actually means some infobodies (e.g., some words in an article), causing you to recall some images in your brain. In this sense, there is actually no "information" existing in the world but all infobodies.

This statement may cause something so-called "cycle definition" because we used "information" to define infobody as "any physical body that contains information is called an infobody," and now we say "information" is actually infobodies. To avoid this antinomy, we can redefine "infobody" as any physical body that can generate an image in a person's brain or cause a person to recall the images existing in his/her brain. These images are generated and stored in his/her brain by his/her sense organs such as eyes, ears, nose, tongue, and skin. However, we still want to keep using the word "information" as all people get used to it.

1.2 Processor and Input and Output Infobodies

Let's use a simple example to think about the process of how a realty infobody is translated into an image in a person's brain. Suppose a person sees a car on the street. That car becomes a reality infobody, and it is processed by his eyes, and an image is generated in his brain. The real process is more complicated than this simplified description, but it can be used to think about the major components in the process.

In this process, there are three major components: input infobody, processor, and output infobody. The car on the street is the input infobody, the person's eyes as a whole are the processor to process the input infobody, and the image generated in his brain is the output infobody.

In this example, we get some concepts about input, processor, and output.

An *infobody processor* is also a physical body that can process one or more input infobodies and generate one or more output infobodies. The input infobody is often simplified as input, and the output infobody is often simplified as output. The infobody processor is often simplified as processor. The single process in which a processor processes the input infobodies and generates the output infobodies is called an *infobody process*.

Please note, a processor must process some input infobodies and must generate some output infobodies. There is no processor that does not process any input infobody or does not generate any output infobodies.

A processor can be a combination of two or more physical bodies. For example, a person using a computer can be considered a single processor.

The output infobodies generated by a processor can become input infobodies for other processors to generate other output infobodies.

1.3 Container Infobody

An infobody can contain one or more infobodies. For example, a book contains many chapters, a chapter contains many sections, a section contains many sentences, and a sentence contains many words. Please note, usually, we do not treat a single character as an infobody because it does not provide enough information unless it is meaningful in some cases. For example, to answer some questionnaires, we may use "Y" to mean "yes" and "N" to mean "no."

A technical example for containers is a database. A database usually contains multiple tables. A table usually contains multiple columns. A column contains multiple values. A table also contains multiple rows. A row also contains multiple values.

A processor can also contain one or more processors. For example, a company has a lot of employees. So all employees compose the company. The company contains many departments, a department contains many teams, a team contains many individual employees. Each employee processes some input infobodies (e.g., some data from a database) and generates some output infobodies (e.g., a few reports).

An infobody that contains other infobodies is often called a *container infobody* or simply a *container*. A container may contain other sub-containers that may contain further sub-containers. At the end of the containing chain, there are some infobodies that do not contain any other infobodies. An infobody that does not contain any other infobodies is called an *atom infobody*.

Similarly, a processor that contains other processors is called a *container processor* or simply a *container*. A processor that does not contain any other processors is called an *atom processor*.

Contained infobodies can also be called *nested* infobodies. A series of nested infobodies is called a *containing chain*.

Please note, a container may contain both infobodies and processors. For example, every human being has a brain storing a lot of images (infobodies). Also, everybody has eyes, ears, nose, tongue, and skin (processors) to process the reality infobodies and generate the infobodies in his/her brain. A technical example is a database that contains data tables (infobodies) and stored procedures (processors). A computer is a container that contains files (infobodies) and software applications (processors). A company is a container that contains employees (processors) and computers (infobodies and processors).

Empty is a specific infobody that is contained in any non-empty infobody.

1.4   Infobody Structure

The processors and the related input and output infobodies and all related containers are called an *infobody structure* as a whole. In general language, it is often called a system, but we use the term infobody structure to emphasize our focus on the infobody containing relationship and the input-output processing relationship. All individual infobodies, processors, and containers in an infobody structure are called *infobody elements*.

Any processor must process some input infobodies and generate some output infobodies. There is no processor that can only generate output infobodies without processing any input infobodies. Also, there is no processor that can only process input infobodies without generating any output infobodies. So an infobody structure is always starting from some input infobodies and ending at some output infobodies.

Theoretically, we can extend an infobody structure endlessly, but we usually focus on a specific cycle of an infobody structure. For example, you find a thermostat is broken in your house. You then search online to find a replacement and order it. After a few days, you receive it, and you install it to replace the broken one. This whole process starts from a reality infobody (broken thermostat) and uses translative infobodies (search online) and ends with a reality infobody (new thermostat). Such an infobody structure starting from a reality infobody and ending at a reality infobody is called a *complete* infobody structure.

A bigger example is a company purchasing a lot of goods from the manufacturers and selling them to the customers. All the activities are recorded in some computer systems. This is also a complete infobody structure starting from the purchased goods (reality infobodies) to the computer system (translative infobodies) and ending at the sold goods (reality infobodies).

Please note, translative infobodies are always involved in any infobody structure, no matter how simple it is. For example, you see an apple (reality infobody) on a table. You see it, so an image (translative infobody) is created in your brain. Then you use your hand to take it (reality infobody).

A single infobody process is the simplest infobody structure. Infobody structure is the main concept we are going to discuss in this book.

1.5   Infobody Expression

In this book, we will use some symbols to denote infobodies and processors and infobody structures. These symbols are called *infobody expressions*. We use brackets ([]) to denote an infobody and use angle brackets (<>) to denote processor and use → to denote input and ⇒ for output.

For example:

$$[\text{infobody 1}] \rightarrow \langle\text{processor 1}\rangle \Rightarrow [\text{infobody 2}] \\ \rightarrow \langle\text{processor 2}\rangle \Rightarrow [\text{infobody 3}] \tag{1.1}$$

We will use dot (.) to denote "contain."

For example,

[infobody 1].[infobody 2].[infobody 3] means [infobody 1] contains [infobody 2] and [infobody 2] contains [infobody 3].

Here is a more complicated technical example (see Figure 1.2 A Nested Infobody Chart):

[container 1].[infobody 1] →
<container 1>.<processor 1> ⇒   (1.2)
[container 2].[infobody 2]

We can also use parentheses for two or more contained infobodies and processors. So (1.2) can also be written as the following:

[container 1].([infobody 1] → <processor 1>) ⇒
[container 2].[infobody 2]   (1.3)

1.6   Infobody Charting

For more complicated infobody structure, infobody expression is hard to write and read. Infobody charting is easier to describe an infobody structure. A good tool for infobody charting is Microsoft Visio, which is a popular charting tool.

Here we will give some simple descriptions of the charting method. More details for infobody charting will be discussed in Chapter 2, "Infobody Charting."

We use rectangular boxes to present infobodies and rounded rectangular boxes to present processors.

The simplest infobody chart is shown in Figure 1.1 below.

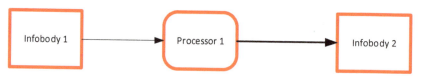

Figure 1.1   A Simple Infobody Chart

In Figure 1.1, the boxes are colored in red, and you can choose any color, but usually, we use the same color for the boxes at the same level in the containing chain. Also, we use a thinner arrow for input and a thicker arrow for output.

Figure 1.2 below shows a little bit more complicated info-body chart with contained infobodies.

As we mentioned before, an infobody can be contained in another infobody as nested infobodies. In the chart, we simply put the infobody box inside the container infobody box with a different color. The same way we can deal with processors. Figure 1.2 shows some nested infobodies and processors.

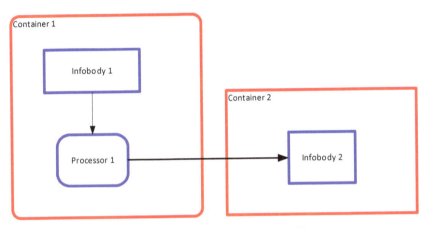

Figure 1.2   A Nested Infobody Chart

Please note a container can contain both infobodies and processors as shown in Figure 1.2.

Figure 1.3 shows a simple infobody chart for person A speaks to person B.

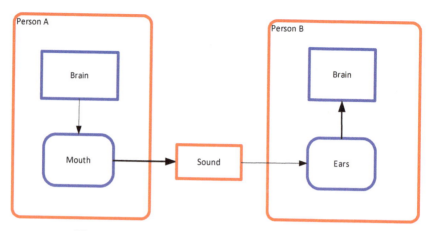

Figure 1.3   Infobody Chart for Conversation

Figure 1.4 shows the process of copy/paste.

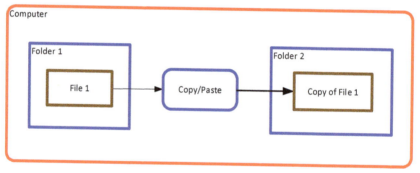

Figure 1.4   Infobody Chart for Copy/Paste

If you are interested in keystrokes, you may chart it as shown in Figure 1.5.

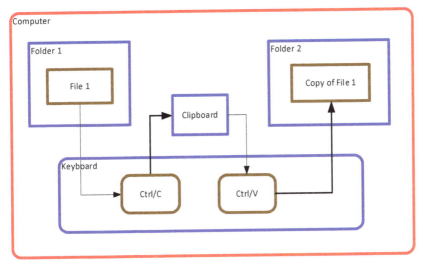

Figure 1.5   Infobody Chart for Copy/Paste with Key Strokes

Please note, we use different colors to distinguish an info-body and its container. The colors are only for the purpose of distinguishing infobodies and no other specific meanings. Usually, we can use the same color for the infobodies at the same level of the containing chain. For example, in Figure 1.5, we used red color for a computer and blue color for the folders and brown for the files. However, we do not have any strict rules for coloring.

When using Visio to make an infobody chart, we often select the "flowchart" chart type. But an infobody chart usually does not really mean any "flow" because in most cases, the physical body does not move to another location, and only a new infobody is created in another location, especially this is true in the computer world. For example, you copy and paste a file from one server to another server. The original file is still in the original server, and only a new file is created by the "copy/paste" processor.

In some special cases, for example, you move a computer from one room to another room. You are moving that infobody (computer), but if you are not interested in the different rooms, you do not need to put the two rooms in your infobody chart as containers.

More details about infobody charting will be discussed in Chapter 2.

1.7   Infobody Model

The infobody charts discussed in Section 1.6 can be regarded as the visual presentation of the infobody model. Here we are going to talk about the infobody model with mathematical terms in graph theory. (Roberts wrote a great book about graph theory and the applications.)

A graph is a relation defined among a number of individual nodes (or vertices). These nodes can present anything like people, computers, buildings, etc. For example, manager A manages two team members, B and C. The "managing" is a relation among these three people: A manages B, and A manages C, but no "managing" relation between B and C. This "managing" relation can be demonstrated as a graph shown in Figure 1.6. The arcs present the managing relation. Arc A to B indicates A manages B. Also arc A to C indicates A manages C.

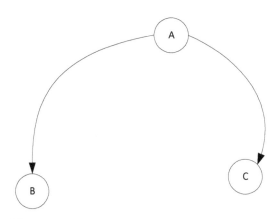

Figure 1.6   A Graph of Managing Relation

Please note the term "graph" and the term "relation" are equivalent. For example, Figure 1.6 can be called a managing relation. It can be called a managing graph as well.

A graph can also be presented as a matrix. For example, the graph in Figure 1.6 can be presented in the matrix below:

$$
\begin{array}{c}
\begin{array}{ccc} A & B & C \end{array} \\
\begin{array}{c} A \\ B \\ C \end{array}
\begin{pmatrix}
0 & 1 & 1 \\
0 & 0 & 0 \\
0 & 0 & 0
\end{pmatrix}
\end{array}
\qquad (1.4)
$$

This matrix is called *adjacency matrix* in graph theory. The number 1 at the entry (A, B) indicates A manages B, and the number 1 at the entry (A, C) indicates A manages C. All zeros indicate no managing relation from the person presented in the row to the person presented in the column. For example, the number 0 at the entry (B, A) indicates B does not manage A. Similarly, the number 0 at the entry (C, B) indicates C does not manage B.

The adjacency matrix provides a way to calculate a graph for various analyses using matrix calculations. The adjacency matrix also makes it possible to store a huge infobody structure into a relational database and so can be queried and calculated using SQL statements or programming languages like Python.

Any infobodies can also be presented as nodes in a graph. The relations between infobodies are more complicated than a single relation like the managing relation in Figure 1.6. In an infobody structure, there are three major relations we are interested in. Let's use the infobody chart in Figure 1.4 as an example to explain our infobody model in terms of graph theory.

First of all, we can see the containing relation between the infobodies. We will use infobody expressions to describe them. In Figure 1.4, [Computer] contains [Folder 1] and [Folder 1] contains [File 1]. In infobody expression, we use dot (.) to present containing relation and so [Computer].[Folder 1].[File 1] becomes a *containing chain*. <Computer>.<Copy/Paste> is another containing chain. The third containing chain is [Computer].[Folder 2].[Copy of File 1]. Note that we use [] for infobody and <> for processor. The container [Computer] contains both infobodies and processors, and so for the containing chain of processors, we denote it as <Computer>.

Note, when we talk about containing chain, the "containing relation" is actually "directly containing relation." For example, the containing chain [Computer].[Folder 1].[File 1] indicates [Computer] directly contains [Folder 1] and [Folder 1] directly contains [File 1]. In fact, [Computer] also contains [File 1], but it is not directly, and so we do not regard [Computer].[File 1] as a containing chain.

A containing chain of infobodies is often simplified as an *infobody chain*, and a containing chain of processors is often simplified as a *processor chain*.

The containing relation indicates the locations of the infobodies. Since infobodies are all physical bodies, they must be located somewhere.

Figure 1.4 also shows the input and output relations. Here we need to separate the input relation and the output relation. The input relation is from the infobodies to the processors, while the output relation is from the processors to the infobodies. Since the infobodies and processors are contained in containing chains, so the input relation is actually defined from the infobody chains to the processor chains, and the output relation is defined from the processor chains to the infobody chains.

In Figure 1.4, the input relation is from the infobody chain [Computer].[Folder 1].[File 1] to the processor chain <Computer>.<Copy/Paste>, and the output relation is from the processor chain <Computer>.<Copy/Paste> to the infobody chain [Computer].[Folder 2].[Copy of File 1]. As we mentioned in Section 1.5 in infobody expressions, we use $\rightarrow$ to denote the input relation and use $\Rightarrow$ to denote the output relation. The whole infobody structure in Figure 1.4 can be denoted in infobody expression as follows:

$$
\begin{aligned}
&[\text{Computer}].[\text{Folder 1}].[\text{File 1}] \rightarrow \\
&<\text{Computer}>.<\text{Copy/Paste}> \Rightarrow \qquad (1.5) \\
&[\text{Computer}].[\text{Folder 2}].[\text{Copy of File 1}]
\end{aligned}
$$

18

Now let's try to denote the infobody structure (1.5) in the matrix format. We need three matrices to present the three relations: containing relation, input relation, and output relation. Let's first take a look at the containing relation. Containing relation is among all infobody elements in the infobody structure, and it means "directly contain." Let's number these elements as follows:

[Computer]	1
[Folder 1]	2
[File 1]	3
<Copy/Paste>	4
[Folder 2]	5
[Copy of File 1]	6

The adjacency matrix of containing relation (graph) can be denoted as below:

$$
\begin{array}{c}
\quad\quad 1\ 2\ 3\ 4\ 5\ 6 \\
\begin{array}{c} 1 \\ 2 \\ 3 \\ 4 \\ 5 \\ 6 \end{array}
\begin{pmatrix}
0 & 1 & 0 & 1 & 1 & 0 \\
0 & 0 & 1 & 0 & 0 & 0 \\
0 & 0 & 0 & 0 & 0 & 0 \\
0 & 0 & 0 & 0 & 0 & 0 \\
0 & 0 & 0 & 0 & 0 & 1 \\
0 & 0 & 0 & 0 & 0 & 0
\end{pmatrix}
\end{array}
\quad (1.6)
$$

Let's use $\mathscr{C}$ to denote this adjacency matrix of the containing relation. It is also called *containing matrix*. Based on this containing relation, we can get the three containing chains:

Infobody Chain A: [Computer].
[Folder 1].[File 1]   or [1.2.3]   (1.7)
Processor Chain B:
<Computer>.<Copy/Paste>   or <1.4>   (1.8)

Infobody Chain C: [Computer].
[Folder 2].[Copy of File 1]   or [1.5.6]   (1.9)

Note, we used three different notations to present containing chains above: a letter, an infobody expression with names, and a simplified infobody expression with numbers. The letters will be used in the adjacency matrices below.

We can get these containing chains directly from matrix (1.6) without looking at Figure 1.4. For example, in matrix (1.6), let's take a look at row 1. The number at entry (1, 2) is 1, meaning 1 contains 2. Then following row 2, we see the number at the entry (2, 3) is 1, meaning 2 contains 3. Then following row 3, all numbers are 0, meaning 3 does not contain any other infobody, which means 3 is an atom infobody. So we can get the containing chain [1.2.3]. Similarly, we can get the other two containing chains <1.4> and [1.5.6]. Notice that we use [] to denote the infobody chain and use <> to denote processor chain.

Note, entry (1,3) is 0 because [Computer] (1) does not directly contain [File 1] (3), and so we do not have containing chain [1.3]. Similarly, entry (1,6) is 0 because [Computer] (1) does not directly contain [Copy of File 1] (6), and so we do not have containing chain [1.6].

Now let's take a look at the input relation in Figure 1.4. The only input relation in Figure 1.4 is [Computer].[Folder 1].[File 1] → <Computer>.<Copy/Paste> or [1.2.3] → <1.4> or A→B. We can also use the adjacency matrix to present this input relation as below:

$$
\begin{array}{c}
B \\
\begin{array}{cc}
A \\
C
\end{array}
\begin{pmatrix}
1 \\
0
\end{pmatrix}
\end{array}
\qquad (1.10)
$$

In this matrix, the number at entry (A, B) is 1 because there is an input relation from infobody chain A to processor chain B. The number at entry (C, B) is 0 because there is no input relation from infobody chain C to processor chain B.

This adjacency matrix (1.10) of the input relation is called *input matrix*, and we denote it as $\mathscr{I}$. Similarly, we can have the adjacency matrix of output relation as follows:

$$B \begin{matrix} A & C \\ \begin{pmatrix} 0 & 1 \end{pmatrix} \end{matrix} \qquad (1.11)$$

In this matrix, the number at entry (B, A) is 0 because there is no output relation from processor chain B to infobody chain A. The number at entry (B, C) is 1 because there is an output relation from processor chain B to infobody chain C. This adjacency matrix (1.11) of the output relation is called *output matrix,* and we denote it as $\mathscr{O}$.

As we mentioned before, a relation is just a graph and can be presented by its adjacency matrix. So matrix $\mathscr{C}$ represents the containing graph that determines all containing chains of all infobodies. Matrix $\mathscr{I}$ represents the input graph, and matrix $\mathscr{O}$ represents the output graph.

Note, the input graph $\mathscr{I}$ and the output graph $\mathscr{O}$ are always paired. Any processor must have at least one input infobody and must have at least one output infobody. So the input relation and the output relation are always paired, with no exceptions. So we put $\mathscr{I}$ and $\mathscr{O}$ together as a paired graph denoted as $\mathscr{I} \sim \mathscr{O}$. This paired graph is based on the set of containing chains determined by the containing graph $\mathscr{C}$.

So the containing graph $\mathscr{C}$ and the paired graph $\mathscr{I} \sim \mathscr{O}$ together as a whole is just our *infobody model*. We give it a specific name in terms of graph theory—*paired graph of chain set,* denoted as ($\mathscr{C}, \mathscr{I} \sim \mathscr{O}$).

The infobody model—paired graph of chain set—can be applied to any infobody structure with millions of infobodies and processors, and the matrices ($\mathscr{C}, \mathscr{I} \sim \mathscr{O}$) provide a way to store the whole infobody structure into a database for calculations and analyses.

We will discuss the infobody model—paired graph of chain set in more detail in Chapter 3 ("Infobody Model in Terms of Graph Theory").

1.8   Chaos and Entropy in Infobody Structure

Chaos and entropy are the concepts from physics (Clausius). In information theory, Shannon also defined the concept of information entropy.

In our infobody theory, we define *chaos* in infobody structures as the *hardness of getting the truth*. The entropy is the numerical measure of the chaos and will be defined later in this section.

What is truth? With infobody concepts, the truth is reality infobodies, which means what is happening or what is existing at a specific location and in a certain time period. So only the people who are at that location and in that time period can see or hear those reality infobodies. Other people never see or hear those reality infobodies, and so hard to know the truth, and they may know it from other people who may hear from someone else.

We can easily see chaos everywhere. In a supermarket, you see the price of a product is $3.49 and so decide to buy it, but you are charged $3.99 when you check out. When you create a report for your manager, your manager says this number is not the same as the other report. You want to buy something online but very hard to find it. Someone committed a crime, but he never admits it. When you run a computer program, it is supposed to get the results in ten seconds, but you wait for ten minutes, still no results. We can make a long list of such things that is very hard to get the truth.

Although there are all kinds of chaos, the key factors are only two in terms of infobody theory: time and credibility.

Let's use some examples to explain these concepts.

Example 1.1   Mailing System

Fifty years ago, if you want to mail a letter to your friend, you need to write the letter on a piece of paper and put it into an envelope and put a stamp on then drop it into a mailbox. The mailman then takes it from the mailbox and puts it in the post office. Then the letter was sent to the airplane, and the plane flies to the destination city, and the mail is sent to the city post office. Then another mailman delivers the letter to the receiver's house. The whole process may need a few days or even a couple of weeks. This process is described in the infobody chart in Figure 1.7.

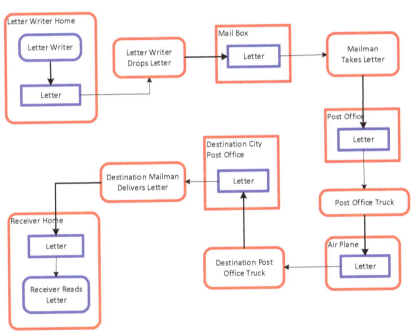

Figure 1.7   Post Office Delivers a Letter

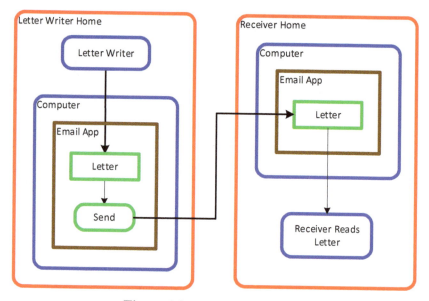

Figure 1.8   Email Processing

In nowadays, we all use emails to do the same thing but much faster (see Figure 1.8). Even better than email, now we all use smartphones to send emails or text messages which is even faster than email because the smartphone is on our hands, so we do not need to open the computers, which takes a longer time.

This example tells us that time is an important and obvious factor in measuring the hardness of getting the truth. The longer time needed, the harder to get the truth. We all know the technical progress can dramatically reduce the hardness of getting the truth.

Example 1.2   Sound "Three" and Symbol "3"

At the beginning of Section 1.1, we described an example about sound "three" and symbol "3." Now let's use an infobody chart to discuss more details.

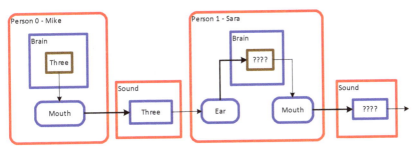

Figure 1.9   Sound "Three" Process

In Figure 1.9, the first person (Person 0 - Mike) thinks about the word "three" in his brain. This is the original source as a reality infobody existing in his brain. Then he uses his mouth to generate a sound infobody "three." Person 1 (Sara) uses her ear in listening to Mike's sound and stores the sound image in her brain. For whatever reasons, the sound she hears might not be "three" and might be "free" or something else. She stores that image in her brain. Then she uses her mouth to generate another sound infobody for whatever is stored in her brain and tells Person 2 (Lisa). Lisa does the same thing as Sara and speaks to Person 3 (John). Suppose at the end for Person 10, he may get "three" or "free" or "tree" or something else. Suppose the probability of getting the correct word is 90 percent for each person, then at the end for Person 10, the probability of getting the correct word is only 35 percent, which means 65 percent probability to get a wrong word. If we extend the number of people to fifty, in the end, the probability of getting the correct word is only 0.5 percent, so the probability of getting a wrong word is 99.5 percent. The probability for getting the truth for a person is called *physical probability* because the reasons are physical for the person's ears or even wind or environmental noises.

Now let's compare it with the case of the symbol "3," which can be described in Figure 1.10 below.

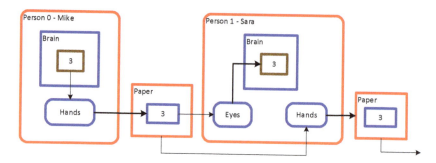

Figure 1.10   Symbol "3" Process

In Figure 1.10, Person 0 (Mike) uses his hands to write the symbol "3" on a piece of paper and then handle it over to Person 1 Sara's hands. Sara uses her eyes to look at the symbol "3" and stores the image in her brain. Then she uses her hands to handle the same piece of paper to Person 2 (Lisa). Lisa does the same thing and handles it to John and so forth. This way, everyone sees the original piece of paper with the symbol "3." At the end of Person 10 (or even Person 50), that person definitely also sees "3," and no one gets wrong. Everyone gets the correct infobody 100 percent (physical probability is 1), so no matter how many people involved, in the end, the last person still gets the correct infobody with a probability of 100 percent = 1:

$$\underbrace{1 \times 1 \times .... \times 1}_{n} = 1^n = 1 \tag{1.12}$$

In this example, we can see the credibility is just the probability of getting the truth.

Example 1.3   Thinking Structure

A boy student in an elementary school stole one dollar from his girl classmate. The teacher asks the boy if he stole the money. The boy thinks about one second and says, "No, I didn't." The teacher then spends one hour talking to the boy and repeatedly emphasizes on "You will not be punished by any means." In the end, the boy acknowledges, "Yes, I did," and returns the money back to the girl.

This process can be charted as in Figure 1.11. In the boy's brain, there is an infobody structure describing his thinking process, and this infobody structure is called *thinking structure*. In his thinking structure, he first said, "No, I didn't," with one-second thinking. This infobody is not the truth. After the teacher spends one hour (3,600 seconds) to keep talking to him with all kinds of advice, especially promises not to punish the boy, eventually, he decides to tell the truth and returns the money to the girl. We call the ratio 1/3600 as *truth ratio*.

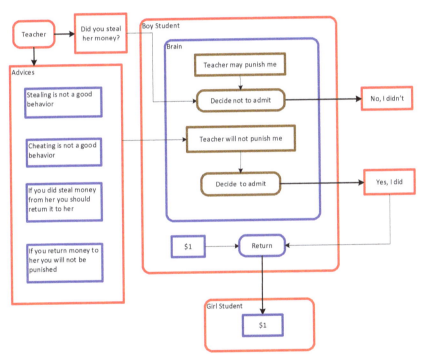

Figure 1.11   Steal Money

We have shown some examples about the chaos. Now let's briefly discuss the concept of entropy.

The measure of chaos is called *entropy*. Figure 1.12 shows a simple infobody structure.

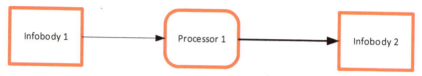

Figure 1.12   A Simple Infobody Structure

Conceptually, we define the entropy of a simple infobody structure as below:

$$E = \frac{T}{C} \qquad (1.13)$$

where E is the entropy, T is the time the processor used to process the input and to generate the output, and C is called *credibility* of the output to the truth.

Note, T is the time to generate the output, but the output may not be the truth. From the three examples above, we can tell some ideas that the credibility is related to the physical probability and the truth ratio. In Chapter 4, we will discuss in much more detail about the chaos and entropy.

1.9   Applications and Research Topics

The infobody theory and infobody model presented in this book is only a starting point for this new academic area and the new technology. There are endless topics for academic research, and endless software and hardware applications can be developed. Here is a list of a few topics and applications out of my mind.

1.9.1   Research Topics

- *Basic Concepts*
  In this book, we presented a lot of basic concepts, but new concepts may be needed when the theory and model are extended.

- *Merge Infobody Structures*
  When two companies are merged together, the two IT systems will need to be merged into a single one. Suppose we have the complete infobody model for each company, then we need to have a method to merge the two infobody models into a single one. There are many topics here that need to be studied.

- *Infobody Structure Simplification*
  Suppose we have an infobody model for a big information system. Getting a sub-infobody model may not be a hard task, but getting a simplified infobody model would be a difficult task. Here, a simplified infobody model means the higher level infobody structure still is a paired graph of chain set.

- *Infobody Structure Drilldown*
  In most cases, an infobody structure should contain all atom infobodies and atom processors, which should not be broken down further. But in some cases, people may want to break an atom infobody or processor into more detailed infobodies or processors. This process is not that hard for infobody charting but not very simple for the graph theory model—paired graph of chain set, so need more research on this topic.

- *Processor Numbering*
  In simple cases, numbering the processors may not be really needed, but for a bigger infobody structure,

numbering processors can help the user to understand the execution order of the processors. But a big infobody structure may have multiple independent input-output paths, numbering the processors can be difficult. Here, the primary serialization rule (from a starting input to number the first processor and then first output then to the second processor and so forth) can be applied to help in this topic.

- *Entropy Definition and Calculation*
   Entropy definition and calculation can be a big topic, especially for credibility definition and calculations. These calculation methods should be applied to do a lot of studies for different countries in the world by specific organizations and announce to the world so people can get more accurate estimates for some major economic or health indicators.

- *Management System Structural Analysis*
   Management system in a company or organization is related to the IT system but not exactly the same. Management system is actually an infobody structure consists of all managers and employees and the communications between them, including computer systems and non-computer systems. Analyzing such an infobody structure is not an easy task, and infobody charting may make it easier.

1.9.2 Software Application Development

- *Infobody Modeler*
   Infobody model can be applied to any infobody structures, especially for complicated information systems in big companies, which may have millions of infobodies and processors. Using infobody charting to chart

30

such huge infobody structures manually is impossible. So there is an obvious need to develop a software application to do most work automatically. I call this software application infobody modeler, and it is not developed yet. It also needs a lot of resources.

The infobody modeler should be able to help any companies and organizations store the infobody structures in databases and generate infobody charts automatically. The infobody modeler should be able to do all kinds of structural analysis for existing system architecture or new system architecture design.

- *Executable Infobody Modeler*

  It should not be very hard to make the infobody modeler executable for a computer system. The processors in an infobody structure can be linked to the executables in the computer system, so clicking on a processor box can start an executable application in the IT system. So the executable infobody modeler can show the progress in the infobody charts just like a big map on the screen to see what is going on in the whole IT system for the company.

- *Cloud Data Collector*

  Infobody modeler itself can be extended to the cloud as a service for any companies and organizations for their own information systems on premise or on the cloud.

  It can also be extended for some federal agencies such as US Census Bureau and Internal Revenue Service to collect data from all individuals and organizations, which will be much more efficient in performance and more accurate in data quality.

- *Online Search Engine*

In nowadays, everyone is using Google as a great search engine to find whatever he or she wants, and many other search engines have been developed. But those search engines are all based on the web pages from the related companies. The existing search engine cannot really search the companies' databases for any detailed information. The infobody model should be able to help for such detailed searches.

- *Dynamic Book*

Currently, in the web pages, we always use hyperlinks to link to other web pages for additional information. But clicking multiple times may make the reader missing connections and hard to get back to the original page.

Based on the infobody model, we should be able to build dynamic books. A dynamic book will be consist of many components. A part of the components can compose a book for a specific topic with necessary base information, and so a reader can select a topic with his or her own knowledge base. In case the reader needs more base knowledge, he or she can click some buttons to get more components adding to the book. So the dynamic book is a personalized book for a specific topic to make the reader easier to understand.

- *Error Handling*

Current error handling in any programming language is not ideal enough to make the developers easy to fix the errors. Most error messages are not detailed enough and almost no suggestions for fixing the errors.

With the infobody model, we should be able to point out any single error at the most detailed level, and so the error messages can be very accurate to the end of the containing chain, and so the solution would also be accurate at that point for the error infobody or processor.

CHAPTER 2

INFOBODY CHARTING

WE WILL PRESENT the formal infobody model in Chapter 3, but that requires some knowledge of graph theory. Before that formal infobody model, we are going to talk about the infobody charting here in this chapter which is a visualization of the formal infobody model and easier to understand, and everyone can use it.

2.1 Infobody Expressions

Even before talking about infobody charting, we will talk about infobody expression first to make the statements easier. Infobody expression defines some symbols to denote the infobodies and processors and the input-output relations.

Table 2.1 shows all symbols and descriptions used in infobody expressions.

Table 2.1   Symbols Used in Infobody Expressions

Symbol	Description	Example
[ ]	Brackets denote an infobody	$[Cusomer]$
< >	Angled brackets denote a processor	$<CopyData>$
→	Single arrow denotes an input relation	$[Customer] \rightarrow <CopyData>$

Table 2.1   (Continued)

$\Rightarrow$	Doubled arrow denotes an output relation	$<CopyData> \Rightarrow [Customer1]$
.	Dot denotes a containing relation	$[Customer].[Sara\,Smith]$
(,)	Parentheses denote multiple infobodies separated by commas contained in a container infobody	$([Customer],[Product])$
:	Colon denotes infobody or processor type	$[Customer:Tbl]$

Usually, we use infobody expressions to describe a simple infobody structure, although it is able to describe a complicated infobody structure. We will use a lot of infobody expressions while talking about infobody charting.

Here is an example of infobody expression for a simple infobody structure:

$$[Customer:Tbl] \rightarrow <CopyData:Sql> \Rightarrow \\ [Customer1:Tbl] \tag{2.1}$$

2.2   Visio for Infobody Charting

The tool we recommend for infobody charting is Microsoft Visio, specifically with [Basic Flowchart Shapes].[Process] and [Miscellaneous Flowchart Shapes].[Dynamic connector]. You may use any other charting tools as far as the tools provide rectangular shape, rounded rectangular shape, and connector as right-angle connector.

Before going into more details, here are some basic settings in Visio for infobody charting:

- *Page Settings*

    Click on [Design].[Page Setup].[↘] to get the [Page Setup] dialog box shown in Figure 2.1:

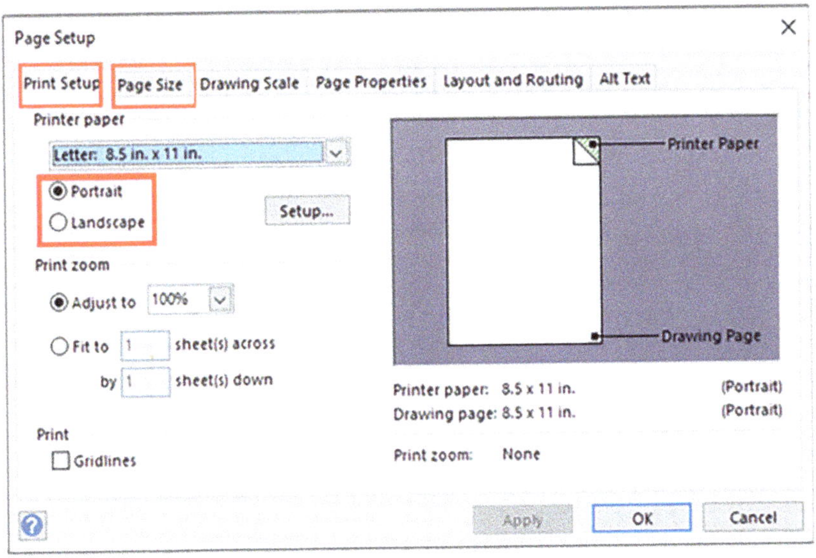

Figure 2.1   [Page Setup] Dialogbox

In [Print Setup].[Printer paper], select [Portrait] or [Landscape] then click [Page Size] to get [Page Size] tab shown in Figure 2.2.

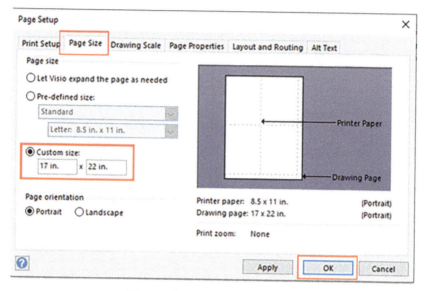

Figure 2.2 [Page Size] Tab

In [Page Size].[Custom size], change 8.5 to 17, and change 11 to 22, then click [OK]. You will get your screen page as 17 in × 22 in. When you print out, you will get four [Letter] pages. You can change the size as you need.

- *Snap and Glue Settings*

    Click on [View].[Visual Aids].[⊠] to get the [Snap & Glue] dialogbox shown in Figure 2.3.

    Select [Currently Active].[Glue] and [Glue to]. ([Shape geometry], [Shape handles], [Shape vertices], [Connection points]) as shown in Figure 2.3.

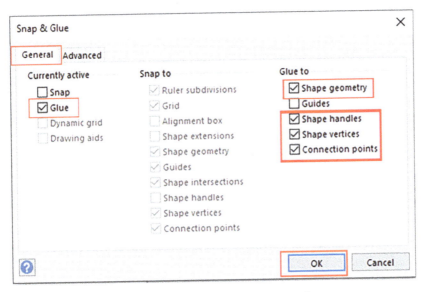

Figure 2.3   [Snap & Glue] Dialogbox

These are recommended settings for infobody charting. You can make any changes as needed.

2.3   Shapes and Connectors

Table 2.2 shows the shapes in Visio and descriptions used in infobody charting.

Table 2.2   Shapes Used in Infobody Charting

Shape	Description	Example
	Rectangular ([Visio].[Basic Flowchart Shapes].[Process]) denotes an infobody	Customer
	Rounded rectangular (Rounding presets 3) denotes a processor	CopyData
→	Thinner (width = 0.5 pt) arrow denotes input relation	Customer → CopyData

Table 2.2   (Continued)

→	Thicker (width = 1.5 pt) arrow denotes output relation	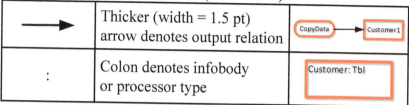
:	Colon denotes infobody or processor type	Customer: Tbl

Note, the line width of all boxes can be set to 3 pt.

Figure 2.4 shows an example of an infobody chart for info-body structure (2.1).

Figure 2.4   Simple Infobody Structure

Note, type is not required as far as the reader can understand.

2.4   Containing and Coloring

Containing relation is an important relation among infobodies and processors. Infobodies are all physical bodies that must take some space to be located, and some infobodies are located inside other infobodies. Some infobodies contain other infobodies. For example, a database contains many tables, a table contains many columns, and a column contains many values. Another example is that a building contains a number of floors, a floor contains a number of rooms, a room contains few computers, a computer contains many folders, and a folder contains many files.

In infobody charting, we can put an infobody box directly inside the containing infobody box to present this containing relation. Figures 2.5 and 2.6 show the two examples mentioned above.

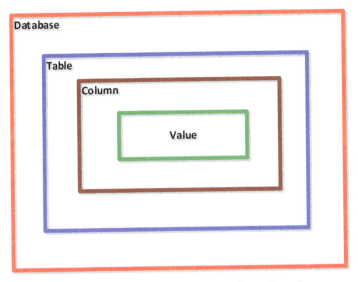

Figure 2.5   Containing Relation for a Database

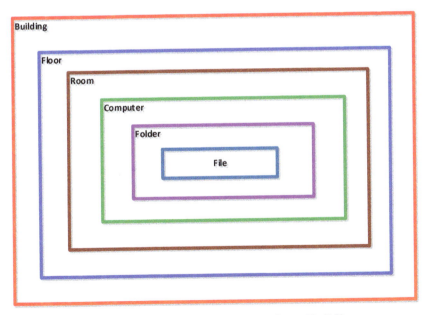

Figure 2.6   Containing Relation for a Building

We recommend using different colors in the containing relations to make it easier to distinguish contained infobodies. Figure 2.7 is a recommended color spectrum for your reference.

Figure 2.7   Containing Relation Color Spectrum

When you need more colors than the colors shown in Figure 2.7, you may use similar colors to the far outer boxes but still with a little difference. There are 16,581,375 choices for the colors, and we never need that many. Usually, containing relations in a single infobody chart would not be more than fifty layers, even for a huge infobody chart.

2.5   Input-Output Charting

Input-output relations are the most important relations in infobody theory. The input relation is from infobodies to processors, and the output relation is from processors to the infobodies, and they are always as paired relations, which means for a certain processor, there must be at least one input infobody and there must be at least one output infobody from that processor.

In an infobody chart, we use a thinner arrow to present an input relation and a thicker arrow to present an output relation. Figure 2.4 in Section 2.3 already showed a pair of simple input relation and output relation.

Below are few examples, and we use these examples to explain the ideas of how to make an infobody chart.

Example 2.1   Post Office Delivers a Letter

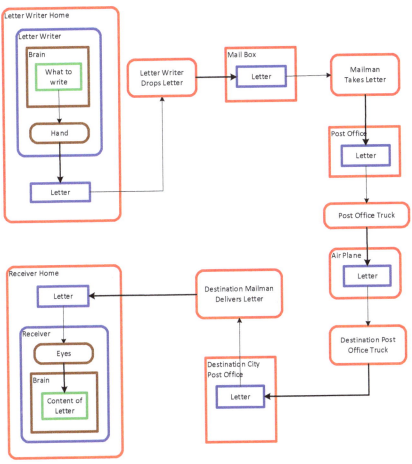

Figure 2.8   Post Office Delivers a Letter

This is a simple and typical example of the physical movement of a reality infobody.

A letter is a reality infobody. It is a piece of paper existing in reality. The letter is generated by the letter writer at his home. His brain contains the content to be written, and he uses his hands to write the letter.

He then takes his letter (enclosed in an envelope) and drops it into a mailbox. This is a physical movement of the letter. The processor is the writer himself, and the input infobody is the letter in his home, and the output infobody is the letter in the mailbox dropped by the writer.

Then the mailman takes the letter from the mailbox and puts it in the post office. Then the post office truck driver takes the letter (in a big package) and drives to the airport, and the airport staff puts the letter package into an airplane.

The airplane flies to the destination city, and the destination post office truck takes the letter package and drives into the destination post office. Finally, the mailman from the destination post office delivers the letter to the receiver's home.

The receiver opens the letter and uses her eyes to read the content of the letter and stores the content in her brain.

Depending on how detailed you want to make the chart, you can chart for each detailed container and processor, or you can omit or combine some containers and processors. For example, you may draw a chart for the letter delivery process as simple as shown in Figure 2.9.

Figure 2.9   Simplified Letter Delivery Structure

From this example, we can get some ideas for charting the physical movement of reality infobodies.

In a physical movement of a reality infobody, the input info-body and the output infobody are the same reality infobody, but it is moved from a physical container to another physical container.

The processor to move a reality infobody must be a person using hands and feet and/or some other tools to move the reality infobody from one place (container) to another.

Example 2.2   Business Management

Figure 2.10 shows a simple business management infobody structure.

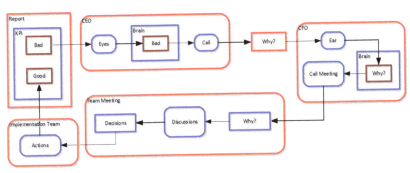

Figure 2.10   Business Management

This infobody structure is about the communications in a business management system. The infobodies are not reality info-bodies but translative infobodies such as report KPI and phone conversations.

When the CEO looks at a report with his eyes, the bad KPI value is generated in his brain. He then calls the CFO and asks why. The CFO hears the question from the CEO with her ears and generates the question in her brain. She then decides to call up a team meeting and asks the same question in the meeting. The attendees have a lot of discussions and make some decisions. These decisions guide the implementation team to take a number of actions for improvement that generate a good KPI value.

All communication infobody structures involve people, and the major processors are human organs such as the eyes, brain, and mouth. When you think about all the details, you can tell what processor processes the input infobody and generates the output infobody. Since a person contains the organs as processors and brain as both storage (images) and processors (thinking), we may use infobody charting to describe the whole thinking structure (will be discussed in Chapter 4, Section 4.4). But for a general communication structure, we may not need to always put the eyes, mouth, and brain in the chart and simply indicate a person as the container for both processors and infobodies. Then Figure 2.10 may be simplified as shown in Figure 2.11.

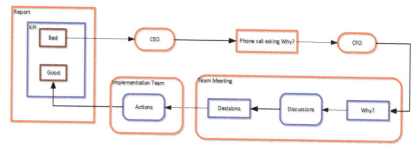

Figure 2.11   Simplified Infobody Chart for Business Management

In terms of infobody theory, usually, the organs in a human body are the atom infobodies such as the brain, eyes, ears, hands, and feet. In some specific cases, you may separate the left hand and right hand and even go down to the fingers level, for instance, which hand finger hits which key in a piano. In most cases, the hand can be regarded as the atom processor. For some communication structures involving many people, like the example above, a person can be regarded as an atom processor. Note, in a human body, there are both infobodies such as the brain and processors such as the eyes. Even the brain can contain both processors (thinking) and infobodies (images). So how to determine the atom infobody and atom processor is based on what level you want to describe in your infobody chart. However, in an infobody chart, the atom level should be consistent.

Example 2.3   TV Show

Figure 2.12 describes a media infobody structure for a TV show.

Suppose there is an event in reality, so everything in the event is a reality infobody, including the speakers, the speeches from the speakers, the audiences, and the repercussions from the audiences.

The whole event is recorded by a video camera from TV Channel X, and some TV clips are generated. The camera reporter put the TV clips into an editing device in the editorial department, and the editor edits the TV clips and makes them as a TV show.

At the time of the TV program in the TV studio of Channel X, the video camera takes the record of the TV host and her commentary, and the edited TV show as well is broadcasted directly to the public. In the home, an audience is watching the television for the TV program on Channel X and stores the contents of the TV program in her brain.

The editing step is the key step. The editor may edit the TV clips based on his idea and even some bias from his political points of view. So what the audiences see may not be exactly the truth. We have some discussions about the thinking structure in Section 4.4.

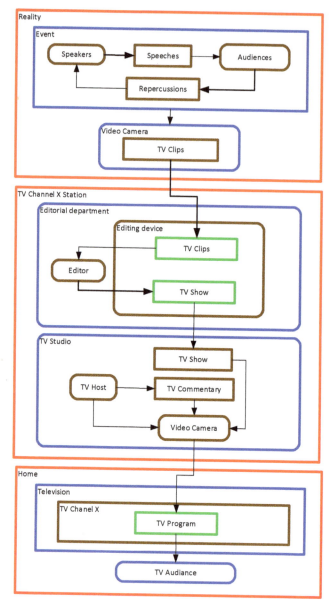

Figure 2.12   TV Show

The examples above are for some infobody structures in our daily lives. The examples below are for computer applications and structures.

Example 2.4   Copy/Paste

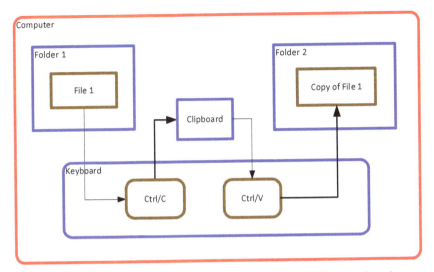

Figure 2.13   Infobody Chart for Copy/Paste with Key Strokes

Copy/paste is the most popular action we take in our computer work as shown in Figure 2.13. Most computer workers understand when we use the ⟨Ctrl/C⟩ keystrokes, we copy [File1] into the clipboard, and so the [Folder1].[File1] is the input infobody, and ⟨Keyboard⟩.⟨Ctrl/C⟩ is the processor, and the [Clipboard] is the output infobody. Then the processor ⟨Keyboard⟩.⟨Ctrl/V⟩ takes the [Clipboard] as the input infobody and generates the output infobody [Folder 2].[Copy of File1].

But some business users may not know there is a clipboard on the computer, and they can only see the keys on the keyboard and see files on the computer screen. So to these users, it may be more understandable to draw a simplified chart like Figure 2.14.

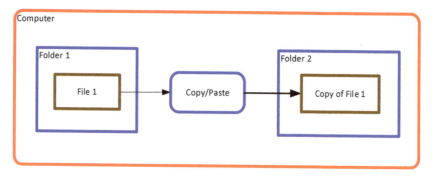

Figure 2.14   Simplified Infobody Chart for Copy/Paste

For charting computer-related infobody structures with a user (person) involved, sometimes, it may not be easy to identify what the input infobody is, what the output infobody is, and what the processor is. The reason for that is the whole process is pretty complicated, and it happens very quickly. For example, a user is typing a Word document. She keeps hitting the keys on the keyboard with her fingers and watching on the screen with her eyes and thinking what to type in her brain, and the text on the screen is growing very fast. Obviously, we do no need to make an infobody chart to describe each keystroke for each letter showing up on the screen. In this case, we may only need to describe the infobody structure as simple as an infobody expression like this:

$$[\text{User}] \rightarrow \langle \text{Keystrokes} \rangle \Rightarrow [\text{Computer}].\,[\text{Word Document}]$$

Note here, the processor ⟨Keystrokes⟩ is a combination of the user's hands and the keyboard. Physically, the hands belong to the human body, and the keyboard is a part of the computer. In this case, we combine hands and keyboard together as a processor outside of the infobody [User] and the infobody [Computer].[Word Document].

Example 2.5   SSIS Package to Calculate Profit Stored Procedure

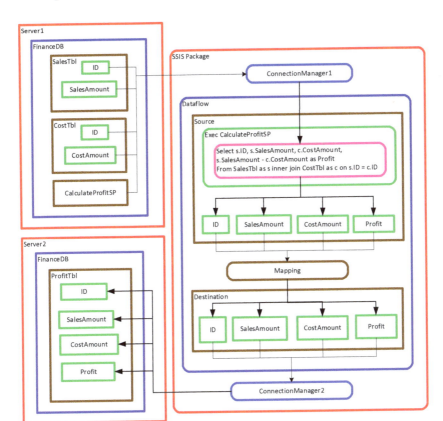

**Figure 2.15   SSIS Calculate a new column
and Move to Another Server**

Figure 2.15 shows an infobody structure for a simple SSIS (SQL Server Integration Services) package. SSIS is a computer application that can move data from one database server to another server. The source data are stored in a database called [FinanceDB] on [Server1]. This database contains two tables called [SalesTbl] and [CostTbl]. The [SalesTbl] table contains two columns called [ID] and [SalesAmount]. The [CostTbl] table contains two columns called [ID] and [CostAmount]. All these servers, databases, tables, and columns are infobodies (or containers) in a containing chain like [Server].[Database].[Table].[Column].

The [FinanceDB] database also contains a stored procedure called [CalculateProfitSP]. Note, this stored procedure is just a piece of SQL code sitting there. It is not running yet, and so it is still an infobody, not a processor.

The SSIS package contains a dataflow. The dataflow defines a source and a destination and a mapping between the source and the destination. Both source and destination are connected to the source database [Server1].[FinanceDB] and the destination database on [Server2].[FinanceDB] through ⟨ConnectionManager1⟩ and ⟨ConnectionManager2⟩.

When this SSIS package is running, the code in the stored procedure ⟨CalculateProfitSP⟩ is executed. Note, we cannot really see anything behind the scenes when the package is running, but we need something to describe it in the chart, and so we use the code to describe it to let the reader understand what is going on. Here we actually use an infobody (the code or the name of the stored procedure) to present the processor.

Example 2.6   Power BI Automatic Calculation

The previous example showed you how to use code to present a processor and show the input infobodies and output infobodies. This example will show you how to present a processor on the screen to generate the output infobody.

Figure 2.16 shows a screenshot in Power BI Desktop. Power BI is a Microsoft tool for creating visualization and dashboard. It is very powerful and easy to use, especially since a lot of calculations are already implemented in the GUI (graphical user interface).

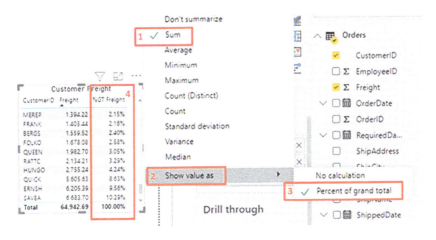

Figure 2.16   Power BI Screenshot for Percent of Grand Total

In this screenshot, we can see ⟨Sum⟩, highlighted in Box 1, ⟨Show value as⟩, highlighted in Box 2, and ⟨Percent of grand total⟩, highlighted in Box 3. Each of these menu items looks like an info-body that we can see on the screen, but when we select them, especially select ⟨Percent of grand total⟩, those selections are telling the application to implement the calculations for ⟨Sum⟩ and ⟨Percent of grand total⟩, and so they are actually processors. The input infobodies are the values of [Freight] column, and the output infobodies are the percentages listed in the [%GT Freight] column in [Customer Freight] table on the Power BI report page.

Figure 2.17 shows the infobody chart for this infobody structure. In the chart, we can see the containing chains and input-output relations like this infobody expression:

$$[\text{Northwind Tabular Model}].[\text{factOrders}].[\text{Freight}] \rightarrow$$
$$\langle 1\,\text{Power BI}\rangle.\langle 2\,\text{Customer Freight Table}\rangle.\langle 3\,\text{Values}\rangle.\langle 4\,\%\text{GT Freight}\rangle.$$
$$\langle 5\,\text{Context Menu}\rangle.\langle 6\,\text{Sum}\rangle \Rightarrow$$
$$\langle 1\cdots 6\rangle.[7\,\text{Sum}:\text{Results}] \rightarrow$$
$$\langle 1\cdots 5\rangle.\langle 6\,\text{Show value as}\rangle.\langle 7\,\text{Percent of grand total}\rangle \Rightarrow$$
$$\langle 1\cdots 2\rangle.[3\,\%\text{GT Freight}] \tag{2.2}$$

In formula (2.2), the infobody expression is pretty complicated, and we used a simplified containing chain like ⟨1···5⟩ to represent the detailed chain ⟨1 Power BI⟩.⟨2 Customer Freight Table⟩.⟨3 Values⟩. ⟨4 %GT Freight⟩.⟨5 Context Menu⟩.

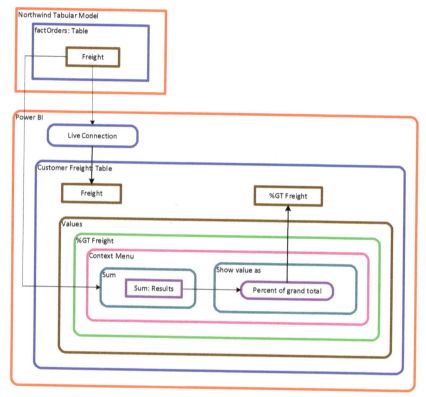

Figure 2.17   Power BI Automatic Calculation

Note, in this chart, ⟨Sum⟩ is a processor that takes the [Freight] column in [factOrders] table as the input infobody and generates the ⌊Sum : Results⌋ as the output infobody. But this is an intermediate result and does not show on the GUI (graphic user interface). Actually, it is in the computer memory, and so we put ⌊Sum : Results⌋ inside of ⟨Sum⟩.

Example 2.7   Empty Infobody

Figure 2.18 shows an example of using empty infobody. A database contains two tables [Table1] and [Table2]. The processor <Delete> deletes [Table2], so [Table2] becomes empty [NULL] that is contained in [Table2] because any infobody contains empty infobody.

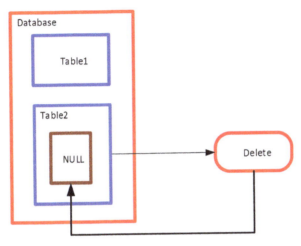

Figure 2.18   Empty Infobody (NULL)

2.6   Mix Charting with Static Relationships

Infobody charting can also be used for describing static relations. ERD (entity relationship diagram) is a popular kind of chart used to describe the relationship between the database tables. If a table has a primary key and another table has a foreign key with the same values, these two tables are considered related with a primary key-foreign key (PK-FK or P-F) relationship, and from the PK table to the FK table, there is a one-to-many relationship, which means for a single PK value in the PK table, there might be multiple FK values in the FK table as the same PK value.

Figure 2.19 shows four tables in a database with some sample data. The first one is called [Orders] that contains columns like [OrderID], [CustomerID], [EmployeeID], [OrderDate], and some other columns. The second table is called [DimDate] that contains columns like [DateKey], [Date], [Year], [Month], [Day], etc. The third one is called [Customers] that contains columns like [CusomerID], [CompanyName], [ContactName], etc. The last one is called [Employees] that contains [EmployeeID], [LastName], [FirstName], [Title], and some other columns.

OrderID	CustomerID	EmployeeID	OrderDate
10248	WILMK	5	7/4/1996 12:00:00 AM
10249	TRADH	6	7/5/1996 12:00:00 AM
10250	HANAR	4	7/8/1996 12:00:00 AM
10251	VICTE	3	7/8/1996 12:00:00 AM

DateKey	Date	Year	Month	Day
19960704	7/4/1996 12:00:00 AM	1996	7	4
19960705	7/5/1996 12:00:00 AM	1996	7	5
19960706	7/6/1996 12:00:00 AM	1996	7	6
19960707	7/7/1996 12:00:00 AM	1996	7	7
19960708	7/8/1996 12:00:00 AM	1996	7	8

CustomerID	CompanyName	ContactName
TRADH	Tradição Hipermercados	Anabela Domingues
TRAIH	Trail's Head Gourmet Provisioners	Helvetius Nagy
VAFFE	Vaffeljernet	Palle Ibsen
VICTE	Victuailles en stock	Mary Saveley
VINET	Vins et alcools Chevalier	Paul Henriot
WANDK	Die Wandernde Kuh	Rita Müller
WARTH	Wartian Herkku	Pirkko Koskitalo
WELLI	Wellington Importadora	Paula Parente
WHITC	White Clover Markets	Karl Jablonski
WILMK	Wilman Kala	Matti Karttunen
WOLZA	Wolski Zajazd	Zbyszek Piestrzeniewicz

EmployeeID	LastName	FirstName	Title
1	Davolio	Nancy	Sales Representative
2	Fuller	Andrew	Vice President, Sales
3	Leverling	Janet	Sales Representative
4	Peacock	Margaret	Sales Representative
5	Buchanan	Steven	Sales Manager
6	Suyama	Michael	Sales Representative

Figure 2.19   Sample Data in Four Tables

From the data in the tables, we can see that the column [OrderID] in table [Orders] contains all unique values (Figure 2.19 only shows four rows) and so it can be set as a primary key (PK). The column [DateKey] or [Date] in table [DimDate] contains all unique values, and so either one of them (but only one) can be set as a primary key (PK), say we set [Date] as the PK. The column [CustomerID] in table [Customers] contains all unique values and so can be set as the PK. Lastly, the column [EmployeeID] in table [Employees] contains all unique values, and so can be set as the PK.

We can see [Orders] table also contains a column called [CustomerID], which is the PK in [Customer] table. Both [CustomerID] columns contain the same values, and for each unique value in [Customer].[CustomerID], there might be multiple the same values in [Orders].[CustomerID]. For example, there are two values of [VICTE] in [Orders].[CustomerID] table actually (not shown in Figure 2.19). This means there is a one-to-many mapping from [Customers].[CustomerID] to [Orders].[CustomerID]. We can set [CustomerID] as a foreign key (FK) in [Orders] table, and we call the one-to-many mapping from [Customers].[CustomerID] to [Orders].[CustomerID] a P-F relationship from [Customers] table to [Orders] table. Similarly, we can set a P-F relationship from [DimDate] table to [Orders] table by the one-to-many mapping from [DimDate].[Date] to [Orders].[OrderDate]. Also, we can set a P-F relationship from [Employees] table to [Orders] table by the one-to-many mapping from [Employees].[EmployeeID] to [Orders].[EmployeeID].

To visualize the P-F relationships, we use a chart called entity relationship diagram (ERD). There are a number of software applications that can create ERD, such as Erwin, Visio, PowerPivot for Excel (free download), and Power BI (free download).

Figure 2.20 shows the ERD for the sample data in Figure 2.19, which is generated in PowerPivot for Excel.

The ERD can also be created by infobody charting—although it is not a software application yet. Figure 2.21 shows the infobody chart for the ERD in Figure 2.20. Here are some differences between Figures 2.20 and 2.21. ERD in Figure 2.21 is at the column level, while the ERD in Figure 2.20 is at the table level.

The ERD in Figure 2.20 contains three P-F relationships at table level:

[DimDate] ⤙ [Orders]

[Customers] ⤙ [Orders]

[Employees]⤙ [Orders]

The ERD in Figure 2.21 contains three P-F relationships at column level:

[DimDate].[Date] ⤙ [Orders].[OrderDate]

[Customers].[CustomerID] ⤙ [Orders].[CustomerID]

[Employees].[EmployeeID] ⤙ [Orders].[EmployeeID]

Note, here we use ⤙ to denote the P-F (one-to-many) relationship in the infobody expressions above while the ERDs in Figures 2.20 and 2.21 use different connectors, but all denote the same P-F (one-to-many) relationships.

Charting ERD at column level is very important to indicate which column is the PK and which column is the FK. For a big database, one table may contain a lot of FKs. In this case, the table level charting is easy to get confused.

Most ERD software applications generate the ERD based on the data in the database, which means you must already have a database and populated with data, while infobody charting can create ERD at the design stage without any data in the database.

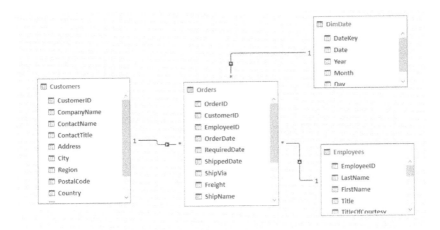

Figure 2.20   Entity Relationship Diagram (ERD)

And furthermore, as you can see in Figure 2.21, infobody charting can have processors to indicate the data sources and the containing chains, while no ERD application can do that. Figure 2.21 also describes the four tables in [DBServer2].[SalesDB] are coming from different sources. The [DBServer2].[SalesDB].[Orders] table is existing in [DBServer2].[SalesDB] while [DBServer2].[SalesDB].[Customers] is coming from [DBServer1].[Customer ManagementDB].[CustomerTbl] by the SSIS package ⟨ImportCustomers⟩. The [DBServer2].[SalesDB].[DimDate] is coming from an Excel spreadsheet [FileServer1].[DateFolder].[Date.xlsx] by the SSIS package ⟨ImportDimDate⟩. The [DBServer2].[SalesDB].[Employees] is coming from a text file [FileServer1].[EmployeeFolder].[Employees.csv].

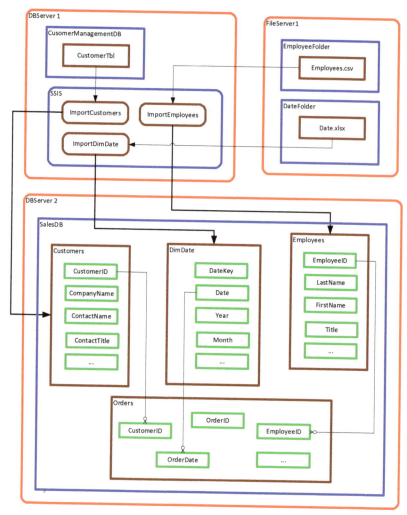

**Figure 2.21   Infobody Chart for Entity
Relationship Diagram (ERD)**

2.7   Path Analysis in Infobody Charting

By highlighting the connectors in a complicated infobody chart, we can trace the paths and so find the data sources as shown in Figure 2.22. However, manually charting a complicated infobody structure is not an easy task, and manually tracing paths is not easy as well.

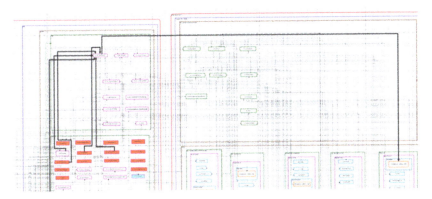

Figure 2.22   Path Analysis in Infobody Charting

To summarize the basic ideas for infobody charting, we want to chart any complicated infobody structure, no matter how sophisticated, how big, how many deep layers, infobody charting should be able to chart it. Figure 2.23 shows an image of a compli-cated infobody chart for a sophisticated web application.

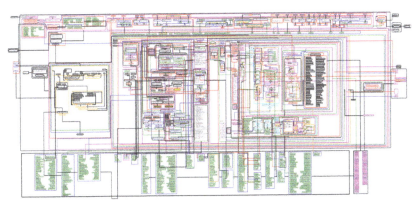

Figure 2.23   An Image of a Complicated Infobody Chart

But realistically, you may consider separating a huge info-body chart into a number of parts and use hyperlinks in Visio to link them together to make each part easier to make and read. You can think of infobody charts as traditional blueprints for manufacturing design. Any small part of a huge machine can be drawn as a blueprint, and any complicated machine can be drawn as blueprints. This is the same idea for infobody charting. As we know, AutoCAD is the software application for blueprints. Unfortunately, there are no similar software applications for infobody charting yet, and that is the direction we want to go. Chapter 3 will present a mathematical model in terms of graph theory which will provide a theoretical base for developing a professional software application for infobody charting and structural analysis.

CHAPTER 3

INFOBODY MODEL IN TERMS OF GRAPH THEORY

IN CHAPTER 2, we talked a lot about infobody charting that already can handle pretty complicated cases with a large number of infobodies. But it is still a manual process and very time-consuming and still limited to a few hundred infobodies. A big infobody structure may contain millions of infobodies which are almost impossible to draw an infobody chart manually, and we must use databases to store so many infobodies, and we need a theoretical model to describe all details in a huge infobody structure. This is what we call the *infobody model*, which is based on the graph theory.

In Chapter 1, Section 1.7, we did talk about the infobody model in terms of graph theory briefly. In this chapter, we will talk about it in much more detail and in a more official format in terms of graph theory.

3.1 Basic Concepts in Graph Theory

We need to briefly mention some basic concepts in graph theory that will be used in our infobody model.

Assume we have two discrete sets, U and V. A relation $\mathscr{R}$ from set U to set V is defined as a subset of the Cartesian product $U \times V$.

A graph $\mathscr{G}$ is defined as a relation $\mathscr{R}$ from set U to set V and denoted as $\mathscr{G}\,(\mathscr{R},\,U,\,V)$.

An important and essential concept in graph theory is the *adjacency matrix* of a graph $\mathscr{G}\,(\mathscr{R},\,U,\,V)$ defined as:

$$\mathscr{A} = \left(a_{ij}\right)_{m \times n} \tag{3.1}$$

where

$$a_{ij} = \begin{cases} 1 & \text{if}\left(u_i, v_j\right) \in \mathscr{R}, \ u_i \in U \text{ and } v_j \in V \\ 0 & \text{if}\left(u_i, v_j\right) \notin \mathscr{R}, \ u_i \in U \text{ and } v_j \in V \end{cases} \tag{3.2}$$

$i = 1,2,\ldots,m$; m is the cardinality of set U
$j = 1,2,\ldots,n$; n is the cardinality of set V

From these definitions, we can understand that graph $\mathscr{G}$ and relation $\mathscr{R}$ and adjacency matrix $\mathscr{A}$ are all equivalent, and so we may use these terms to mean the same thing in different contexts.

When set U and set V are the same, the relation $\mathscr{R}$ is actually defined on a single set U. The graph $\mathscr{G}$ is usually visualized by nodes or vertices (small circles) to present the elements in set U and arcs or edges (with arrows) to present the relation between the nodes. Figure 3.1 shows a simple graph.

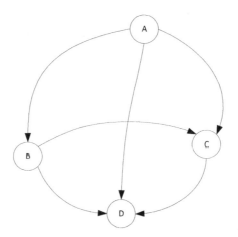

Figure 3.1   A Simple Graph

In this graph, the node-set U contains four nodes, A, B, C, and D, and the relation $\mathscr{R}$ contains six arcs, (A, B), (A, C), (A, D), (B, C), (B, D), and (C, D). The adjacency matrix is

$$A = \begin{array}{c} \\ A \\ B \\ C \\ D \end{array} \begin{array}{cccc} A & B & C & D \\ \begin{pmatrix} 0 & 1 & 1 & 1 \\ 0 & 0 & 1 & 1 \\ 0 & 0 & 0 & 1 \\ 0 & 0 & 0 & 0 \end{pmatrix} \end{array} \qquad (3.3)$$

In a graph, a series of arcs is called a *path* if the end node of each arc is the start node of the next arc. In the graph of Figure 3.1,

$$(A, B), (B, C), (C, D) \qquad (3.4)$$

is a path. The number of arcs in a path is called the *length* of the path. For example, the length of path (3.4) is 3. To simplify a path, we can also use arrows between the nodes, so path (3.4) can be simplified as

$$A \rightarrow B \rightarrow C \rightarrow D$$

3.2 Containing Relation between Infobodies

In Chapter 1, we described the basic concepts: infobody and atom infobody, processor and atom processor, and container. Let's use U to denote the set of all infobody elements in consideration, including atom infobodies, atom processors, and containers. Set U is often called the *universe* of all infobody elements in consideration.

A *containing relation* (denoted as $\mathscr{C}_R$) between the infobody elements in set U is defined as:

$$\mathscr{C}_R = \{(u_i, u_j) \text{ if } u_i \text{ directly contains } u_j \text{ where } (u_i, u_j) \in U \times U\}. \quad (3.5)$$

This is equivalent to the adjacency matrix called *containing matrix* (denoted as $\mathscr{C}_A$):

$$\mathscr{C}_A = \left(c_{ij}\right)_{m \times m} \tag{3.6}$$

where

$$c_{ij} = \begin{cases} 1 & \text{if } (u_i, u_j) \in \mathscr{C}_R, \ u_i \text{ and } u_j \in U \\ 0 & \text{if } (u_i, u_j) \notin \mathscr{C}_R, \ u_i \text{ and } u_j \in U \end{cases} \tag{3.7}$$

$i, j = 1, 2, \ldots, m$; m is the cardinality of set U

The equivalent graph is called *containing graph* denoted as $\mathscr{C}_G(\mathscr{C}_R, U)$.

As we have already seen in Chapter 2 (Infobody Charting), we use rectangles to visualize the infobodies, processors, and containers instead of the nodes (small circle) as in graph theory. The containing relation is presented very clearly by putting a box inside another box.

Why do we need to think about the containing relation? Why not simply use the individual infobodies and processors? The basic reason is that our language is very limited, and so the same term is used in many places for different people and things. For example, the name John Smith may be used by millions of people in the world, so we must specify a containing chain (next section) to identify this John Smith who is not the other John Smiths.

3.3 Containing Chain and Containing Hierarchy

A path in the containing graph $\mathscr{C}_G(\mathscr{C}_R, U)$ is called a *containing path*. A containing path is called a *containing chain* if the end node is an atom infobody (denoted as Ib) or atom processor (denoted as Pr).

Figure 3.2 shows a simple containing graph.

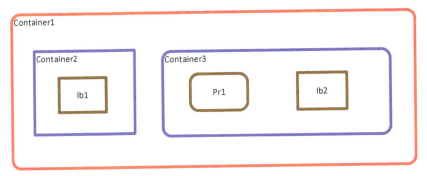

Figure 3.2   A Simple Containing Graph

In this graph, we have three containing chains:

[Container1].[Container2].[Ib1]
<Container1>.<Container3>.<Pr1>
[Container1].[Container3].[Ib2]

Note, [Container1].[Container2] is not a containing chain because the end node [Container2] is not an atom (Ib or Pr). Also note, [Container1] directly contains [Container2], but [Container1] does not directly contain [Ib1].

Figure 3.3 shows a simplified database system.

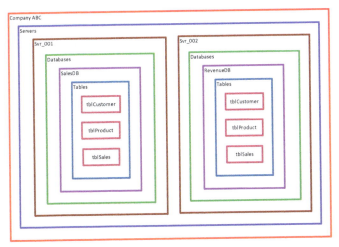

Figure 3.3   A Database System

Below are the six containing chains in this graph:

[Company ABC].[Servers].[Svr_001].[Databases].
[SalesDB].[Tables].[tblCusomer] (3.8)
[Company ABC].[Servers].[Svr_001].[Databases].
[SalesDB].[Tables].[tblProduct] (3.9)
[Company ABC].[Servers].[Svr_001].[Databases].
[SalesDB].[Tables].[tblSales] (3.10)
[Company ABC].[Servers].[Svr_002].[Databases].
[RevenueDB].[Tables].[tblCusomer] (3.11)
[Company ABC].[Servers].[Svr_002].[Databases].
[RevenueDB].[Tables].[tblProduct] (3.12)
[Company ABC].[Servers].[Svr_002].[Databases].
[RevenueDB].[Tables].[tblSales] (3.13)

In these containing chains, we see some containers like [Servers], [Databases], and [Tables]. We call such a container *collective container* because it means a collection of the individual infobodies contained in the collection, and the individual infobodies usually have different names such as [SalesDB] and [RevenueDB]. The universe is also a collective container.

Note, the collective container [Databases] in chain (3.8) is different from the collective container [Databases] in chain (3.11). One is in [Svr_001], containing database [SalesDB], and the other one is in [Svr_002], containing database [RevenueDB]. In the containing graph, they are different nodes. That is the basic reason why we have to use a containing chain to identify an infobody because many different infobodies may have exactly the same name. For the same reason, the table [tblProduct] in (3.9) is different from the table [tblProduct] in (3.12).

Also, we need to keep in mind that all infobodies we are talking about are in the same universe U, [Company ABC] in this example, not in the world. If we take the world as the universe, there might be thousands of people with the same name, such as [John Smith], and we may need to use a long containing chain to identify each individual [John Smith].

We can create a *virtual infobody* (not existing in the universe *U*) to represent each individual named infobody. For example, we can create a virtual container [Each Database] to represent [SalesDB] or [RevenueDB] but not both. Such a virtual infobody is called a *representative infobody*. If we replace the individual named infobodies with the representative infobodies, the six containing chains, (3.8) – (3.13), will become a single one:

[Company ABC].[Servers].[Each Server].[Databases].
[Each Database].[Tables].[Each Table]   (3.14)

The infobody expression (3.14) is called the *containing hierarchy* that can be applied to the six containing chains, (3.8)–(3.13). From this example, we can see a containing hierarchy is an abstracted pattern that can be applied to a group of containing chains.

Each infobody (collective and representative) in a hierarchy is called a *level*, and we usually number the levels in the same order as in the hierarchy. So the hierarchy (3.14) has seven levels:

$$L_0 . L_1 . L_2 . L_3 . L_4 . L_5 . L_6 \qquad (3.15)$$

The expression (3.15) is called *level* series. The number of levels in a hierarchy is called the *length* of the hierarchy. So the length of the hierarchy (3.14) is 7.

Note, we used L_0 to denote the universe U = [Company ABC]. In most cases, we do not need to include the universe in a containing chain or containing hierarchy. For containing chain, (3.8) can be written as:

[Servers].[Svr_001].[Databases].[SalesDB].
[Tables].[tblCusomer]   (3.16)

and the containing hierarchy (3.14) can be written as:

[Servers].[Each Server].[Databases].[Each Database].
[Tables].[Each Table]   (3.17)

and the level series (3.15) can be written as:

$$L_1 . L_2 . L_3 . L_4 . L_5 . L_6 \qquad (3.18)$$

The length becomes six for each of them.

As we have seen in Chapter 2 (Infobody Charting), we use the same color for the infobodies at the same level in the containing hierarchies.

Note, if not confusing, sometimes, the collective containers can be omitted as far as understandable. For example, (3.14) can be simplified as:

[Company ABC].[Each Server].[Each Database].
[Each Table]   (3.19)

with four levels, and it can be applied to a simplified chain:

[Company ABC].[Svr_001].[SalesDB].[tblCusomer]   (3.20)

But (3.19) cannot be applied to a containing chain like this:

[Company ABC].[SWC0012].[TPK35].[HAM0967]   (3.21)

because in containing chain (3.21), we do not even know what [SWC0012], [TPK35], and [HAM0967] are. The expression (3.20) tells us if we want to omit some collective containers, we need to use some letters (such as Svr, DB, tbl) to indicate the omitted collective container in the individual containers.

3.4   Intersectional Hierarchies

In some cases, it may not be easy to determine the containing hierarchy. Table 3.1 shows a matrix:

Table 3.1   Sample Matrix

	Customer 1	Customer 2	Customer 3
Product 1	1	2	3
Product 2	4	5	6

Note, a matrix is different from a table in a database. A database table contains named columns but no names for the rows, and some columns contain text values or even pictures or binary values. But a matrix contains named columns and named rows, and the intersection of each column and each row contains only numbers. In a database, we may use SQL pivot statement to create a matrix (also called pivot table or crosstab table).

In a matrix, the collective container of columns or rows is called a *dimension*. In Table 3.1, the three columns can be collectively called [Customer Dimension] or [dimCusomer], and the two rows can be collectively called [Product Dimension] or [dimProduct]. The containing hierarchy can be written as:

[Matrix].[Dimensions].[EachDimension].[Members].
[EachMember].[Values]   (3.22)

Let's take a look at two specific containing chains:

[Matrix].[Dimensions].[dimCustomer].[Members].
[Customer3].[6]   (3.23)

and

[Matrix].[Dimensions].[dimProduct].[Members].
[Product2].[6]   (3.24)

These two chains contain the same atom value [6] at the intersection of [Customer3] and [Product2], but these two chains both are missing one container. The chain (3.23) is missing [dimProduct] while (3.24) is missing [dimCustomer], and we cannot tell the atom value [6] is at the intersection of [Customer3] and [Product2]. That means we need to keep both dimensions in the hierarchy, which may yield two different hierarchies:

[Matrix].[Dimensions].[dimCustomer].[Members].
[Customer3].[RestDimensions].[dimProduct].
[Members].[Product2].[Value]   (3.25)

[Matrix].[Dimensions].[dimProduct].[Members].
[Product2].[RestDimensions].[dimCustomer].
[Members].[Customer3].[Value]   (3.26)

These two hierarchies are intersectional with a common info-body [Value]. Note, the collective container [RestDimensions] in (3.25) is different from the collective container [RestDimensions] in (3.26). The former one means the rest dimensions other than [dimCustomer], and the latter one means the rest dimensions other than [dimProduct].

These two hierarchies tell us that we need to determine an order for the dimensions for a unique hierarchy. The order can be any order but must be unique. In our example, we can take (3.25) as the unique hierarchy.

We can imagine if we have many dimensions (e.g., a multidimensional cube with ten dimensions), the hierarchy (3.25) would be very long. We can use the following format to describe a multidimensional containing hierarchy:

$$[Cube].[Dim_1] \times [Dim_2] \times ... \times [Dim_n].[Value] \qquad (3.27)$$

where $[Dim_1] \times [Dim_2] \times ... \times [Dim_n]$ is the Cartesian product of n dimensions. Sometimes, it can be written as

$$\prod_{i=1}^{n} [Dim_i] \qquad (3.28)$$

and so (3.27) can be simplified as

$$[Cube].\prod_{i=1}^{n}[Dim_i].[Value] \qquad (3.29)$$

Another example of intersectional hierarchies is for location and organization. One employee is located in a building on a floor in an area in a cubicle in the following location hierarchy:

[Company].[Buildings].[EachBuilding].[Floors].
[EachFloor].[Areas].[EachArea].[Cubicles].
[EachCubicle].[OneEmployee]   (3.30)

The same employee can be also organized in the organization hierarchy:

[Company].[Departments][EachDepartment].[Teams].
[EachTeam].[Employees].[EachEmploee]   (3.31)

These two hierarchies not only have an intersection at the end for an employee but also may have intersections at any other levels. For instance, one building may have multiple departments, and one department may be in multiple buildings. In this case, we can merge two or more hierarchies into a single one in a certain order, just like a multidimensional cube. For instance, hierarchy (3.30) and (3.31) may be merged into a single hierarchy like this:

[Company].[Buildings].[EachBuilding].[Departments]
[EachDepartment].[Floors].[EachFloor].
[Areas].[EachArea].[Teams].[EachTeam].[Emplyees].
[EachEmployee]   (3.32)

This can also be simplified as:

[Company].[EachBuilding].[EachDepartment].
[EachFloor].[EachArea].[EachTeam].
[EachEmployee]   (3.33)

In an infobody model, we never need to list all values as atom infobodies. For example, in a database table with millions of rows, we never need to list all these millions of values as the atom infobodies and so all millions of containing chains in the model. How to determine the atom infobodies depends on the model purpose. Also, an atom can be changed to a container by adding more infobodies into it if necessary.

3.5 Input-Output Paired Relations

All containing chains compose a set called *chain set*, denoted as CS. The chain set CS can be divided into two parts, Ib chains and Pr chains. An *Ib chain* is a containing chain with an Ib (atom infobody) as the end node. A *Pr chain* is a containing chain with a Pr (atom processor) as the end node. All Ib chains compose a subset of CS called *Ib chain set*, denoted as BC. All Pr chains compose another subset of CS called *Pr chain set*, denoted as PC.

A Pr (atom processor) must have at least one input Ib (atom infobody) and at least one output Ib. But an atom can only be identified in a containing chain, and so the input and output relations need to be defined on the chain sets.

The *input relation* (denoted as $\mathscr{I}_R$) from the Ib chain set BC to the Pr chain set PC is defined as:

$$\mathscr{I}_R = \{(bc_s, pc_t) \text{ if the atom Ib in } bc_s \text{ is an input}$$
infobody to the atom Pr in pc_t
where $(bc_s, pc_t) \in BC \times PC\}$ $\qquad (3.34)$

This is equivalent to the adjacency matrix called *input matrix* (denote as $\mathscr{I}_A$):

$$\mathscr{I}_A = (d_{st})_{m \times n} \qquad (3.35)$$

where

$$d_{st} = \begin{cases} 1 & \text{if } (bc_s, pc_t) \in \mathscr{I}_R, \ bc_s \in BC \text{ and } pc_t \in PC \\ 0 & \text{if } (bc_s, pc_t) \notin \mathscr{I}_R, \ bc_s \in BC \text{ and } pc_t \in PC \end{cases} \qquad (3.36)$$

$s = 1, 2, \ldots, m$; m is the cardinality of set BC

$t = 1, 2, \ldots, n$; n is the cardinality of set PC

The equivalent graph is called *input graph*, denoted as $\mathscr{I}_G(\mathscr{I}_R, U)$.

We can define output relation in a similar way.

The *output relation* (denoted as $\mathscr{O}_R$) from the Pr chain set PC to the Ib chain set BC is defined as:

$\mathscr{O}_R = \{(pc_t, bc_s)$ if the atom Ib in bc_s is an output infobody from the atom Pr in pc_t

where $(pc_t, bc_s) \in PC \times BC\}$ $\hfill$ (3.37)

This is equivalent to the adjacency matrix called *output matrix* (denoted as $\mathscr{O}_A$):

$$\mathscr{O}_A = (f_{ts})_{n \times m} \hfill (3.38)$$

where

$$f_{ts} = \begin{cases} 1 & \text{if } (pc_t, bc_s) \in \mathscr{O}_R, \ pc_t \in PC \text{ and } bc_s \in BC \\ 0 & \text{if } (pc_t, bc_s) \notin \mathscr{O}_R, \ pc_t \in PC \text{ and } bc_s \in BC \end{cases} \hfill (3.39)$$

$t = 1, 2, \ldots, n$; n is the cardinality of set PC

$s = 1, 2, \ldots, m$; m is the cardinality of set BC

The equivalent graph is called *output graph*, denoted as $\mathscr{O}_G(\mathscr{O}_R, U)$.

Note, the input relation and the output relation defined here are two separate relations. These two relations have a specific relation. As we mentioned before, any atom processor Pr must have at least one input atom infobody Ib and at least one output Ib, which means for any single arc (bc_{s_1}, pc_{t_0}) with the end node pc_{t_0} in the input graph $\mathscr{I}_G$ there must be at least one arc (pc_{t_0}, bc_{s_2}) with the same node pc_{t_0} in the output graph $\mathscr{O}_G$.

In terms of adjacency matrix, if there is a 1 in column t_0 in the input matrix $\mathscr{I}_A$, then there must be at least one 1 in row t_0 in the output matrix $\mathscr{O}_A$.

The arc $\left(bc_{s_1}, pc_{t_0}\right)$ in $\mathscr{I}_G$ and the arc $\left(pc_{t_0}, bc_{s_2}\right)$ in $\mathscr{O}_G$ are called *paired arcs with* pc_{t_0}. This bc_{s_1} is called an *input chain to* pc_{t_0}, and bc_{s_2} is called an *output chain from* pc_{t_0}. Note, there might be multiple input chains and output chains for a single Pr chain pc_{t_0}. The input graph $\mathscr{I}_G$ and the output graph $\mathscr{O}_G$ are called *paired graphs*, and we regard them as a single combined graph just called *paired graph*, denoted as $\mathscr{I}_G \sim \mathscr{O}_G$.

3.6 Infobody Model

We need to remember, a node in the paired graph $\mathscr{I}_G \sim \mathscr{O}_G$ is a containing chain defined in the containing graph $\mathscr{C}_G$, so the paired graph $\mathscr{I}_G \sim \mathscr{O}_G$ is based on the containing graph $\mathscr{C}_G$. The combination of these three graphs is called a *paired graph of chain set*, which is just our *infobody model* in terms of graph theory and is denoted as ($\mathscr{C}_G, \mathscr{I}_G \sim \mathscr{O}_G$).

As we already know, a graph is equivalent to the based-on relation and also equivalent to the adjacency matrix. So we can also present an infobody model in the form of relation as ($\mathscr{C}_R$, $\mathscr{I}_R \sim \mathscr{O}_R$) or in the form of adjacency matrix ($\mathscr{C}_A, \mathscr{I}_A \sim \mathscr{O}_A$). To simplify, we can denote an infobody model as ($\mathscr{C}, \mathscr{I} \sim \mathscr{O}$), and remember, it has three forms in the graph, relation, and adjacency matrix respectively. We will use them accordingly based on the context. The infobody model can be applied to any infobody structure.

3.6.1 Paths in Infobody Model

In an infobody model, ($\mathscr{C}_G, \mathscr{I}_G \sim \mathscr{O}_G$), $\mathscr{C}_G$ is the containing graph for identifying the atom Ibs and Prs that we have discussed in detail in Sections 3.2–3.4. Now we will discuss more about $\mathscr{I}_G \sim \mathscr{O}_G$, the paired input-output ($I \sim O$) graph.

An arc series:

$$\left(bc_1, pc_1\right), \left(pc_1, bc_2\right), \left(bc_2, pc_2\right), \left(pc_2, bc_3\right), \cdots$$
$$\left(bc_{n-1}, pc_{n-1}\right), \left(pc_{n-1}, bc_n\right) \qquad (3.40)$$
$$n = 2, 3, \ldots$$

is called a path in the $I{\sim}O$ graph. The number of arcs in the path is called the *length* of the path, denoted as *Len*. The length of path (3.40) is:

$$Len = 2\,(n-1) \qquad (3.41)$$

Since every containing chain has an atom (Ib or Pr) and the input and output are actually for the atoms, (3.40) can be simplified using infobody expressions as follows:

$$Ib_1 \rightarrow Pr_1 \Rightarrow Ib_2 \rightarrow Pr_2 \Rightarrow Ib_3 \cdots Ib_{n-1} \rightarrow Pr_{n-1} \Rightarrow Ib_n \qquad (3.42)$$

Path is a primary concept for any infobody model analysis. Since the infobody model is not a usual graph, the paths in the infobody model are also different from the paths in usual graph as well as path analysis.

3.6.2 Paired Adjacency Matrices

In the adjacency matrix form of the infobody model ($\mathscr{C}_A$, $\mathscr{I}_A{\sim}\mathscr{O}_A$), $\mathscr{I}_A{\sim}\mathscr{O}_A$ are the paired adjacency matrices, which is the primary base for any infobody model analysis because they describe the complete infobody structure with numbers (1 and 0), and numbers are the very basic tool for calculations. They are simply called *I~O matrices,* and $\mathscr{I}_A$ is the input matrix, and $\mathscr{O}_A$ is the output matrix.

The input matrix $\mathscr{I}_A = \left(d_{st}\right)_{m \times n}$ describes the input relation from Ibs to Prs. Each row represents an Ib, and each column represents a Pr. The sum of all rows for each column t is called the *column sum* for column t of the input matrix, denoted as

$CSum_t(\mathscr{I}_A) = \sum_{s=1}^{m} d_{st}$ $t = 1, 2, \ldots n$ and n is the number of columns (Prs) $\hspace{2cm}$ (3.43)

$CSum_t(\mathscr{I}_A)$ indicates the number of atom Ibs that are the inputs to atom Pr t.

The sum of all columns for each row s is called the *row sum* for row s of the input matrix, denoted as

$RSum_s(\mathscr{I}_A) = \sum_{t=1}^{n} d_{st}$ $s = 1, 2, \ldots m$ and m is the number of rows (Ibs) $\hspace{2cm}$ (3.44)

$RSum_s(\mathscr{I}_A)$ indicates the number of atom Prs that take Ib s as inputs.

Similarly, we can define the column sum and row sum for the output matrix $\mathscr{O}_A = (f_{ts})_{n \times m}$ as follows:

$CSum_s(\mathscr{O}_A) = \sum_{t=1}^{n} f_{ts}$ $s = 1, 2, \ldots m$ and m is the number of columns (Ibs) $\hspace{2cm}$ (3.45)

$CSum_s(\mathscr{O}_A)$ indicates the number of atom Prs that generate Ib s as output.

$RSum_t(\mathscr{O}_A) = \sum_{s=1}^{m} f_{ts}$ $t = 1, 2, \ldots n$ and n is the number of rows (Prs) $\hspace{2cm}$ (3.46)

$RSum_t(\mathscr{O}_A)$ indicates the number of atom Ibs that are generated by Pr t.

These row and column sums can indicate some nature of the Ibs and Prs, and we summarize them as follows:

$RSum_s(\mathscr{I}_A) = 0$ indicates that the atom Ib for row s is not an input to any atom Pr, which means this Ib is an *ending* Ib in the infobody model. $\hspace{1cm}$ (3.47)

$CSum_s(\mathcal{O}_A) = 0$ indicates that the atom Ib for column s is not an output from any atom Pr, which means this Ib is a *starting* Ib in the infobody model. (3.48)

Also note, $RSum_t(\mathcal{O}_A) = 0$ can never happen for any row t (Pr) because any atom Pr must have at least one output Ib. Similarly, $CSum_t(\mathcal{I}_A) = 0$ can never happen because any atom Pr must have at least one input Ib.

3.7   IPO Table

Input and output (I~O) matrices $\mathcal{I}_A$ and $\mathcal{O}_A$ are useful but not easy for infobody model path analysis because path analysis needs to use matrix multiplications many times. The input and output matrices themselves are already huge for a big infobody structure. The matrix multiplications for a huge number of times would need a huge amount of computer resources. Additionally, the I~O matrices are both huge sparse matrices, meaning most entries are 0s that are not necessary to keep and occupy the computer resources.

Here we present a new way to simplify the methods for infobody model path analysis. From the I~O matrices, we can create a table similar to the database table with three columns: I for input Ibs, P for atom Prs, and O for output Ibs. This table is called *IPO table*. Table 3.2 shows a general IPO table.

Table 3.2   General IPO Table

I	P	O
$Ib_{11}^{(I)}$	Pr_1	$Ib_{11}^{(O)}$
$Ib_{21}^{(I)}$	Pr_1	$Ib_{12}^{(O)}$
$\vdots$	$\vdots$	$\vdots$

Table 3.2   (Continued)

$Ib^{(I)}_{m_1 1}$	Pr_1	$Ib^{(O)}_{1m_1}$
$\vdots$	$\vdots$	$\vdots$
$Ib^{(I)}_{1t}$	Pr_t	$Ib^{(O)}_{t1}$
$\vdots$	$\vdots$	$\vdots$
$Ib^{(I)}_{st}$	Pr_t	$Ib^{(O)}_{ts}$
$\vdots$	$\vdots$	$\vdots$
$Ib^{(I)}_{m_t t}$	Pr_t	$Ib^{(O)}_{tm_t}$
$\vdots$	$\vdots$	$\vdots$
$Ib^{(I)}_{1n}$	Pr_n	$Ib^{(O)}_{n1}$
$Ib^{(I)}_{2n}$	Pr_n	$Ib^{(O)}_{n2}$
$\vdots$	$\vdots$	$\vdots$
$Ib^{(I)}_{m_n n}$	Pr_n	$Ib^{(O)}_{nm_n}$

In Table 3.2:

Pr_t is the t-th atom Pr.

The set $\left\{ Ib^{(I)}_{1t}, \ldots, Ib^{(I)}_{st}, \ldots, Ib^{(I)}_{m_t t} \right\}$ is the input Ib set to Pr_t with m_t atom Ibs.

The set $\left\{ Ib^{(O)}_{t1}, \ldots, Ib^{(O)}_{ts}, \ldots, Ib^{(O)}_{tm_t} \right\}$ is the output Ib set from Pr_t with m_t atom Ibs.

Note, both input set and output set may have empty Ibs (NULLs as in a database), and so they may not have the same number of Ibs.

Figure 3.4 is a sample infobody structure that will be used to demonstrate all theoretical descriptions in an infobody model.

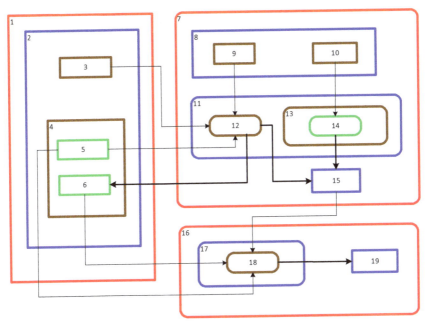

Figure 3.4   Sample Infobody Structure

In this infobody structure, we have the containing chains listed below:

bc1: [1].[2].[3]	([3] is an atom Ib)
bc2: [1].[2].[4].[5]	([5] is an atom Ib)
bc3: [1].[2].[4].[6]	([6] is an atom Ib)
bc4: [7].[8].[9]	([9] is an atom Ib)
bc5: [7].[8].[10]	([10] is an atom Ib)

bc6: [7].[15]	([15] is an atom Ib)
bc7: [16].[19]	([19] is an atom Ib)
pc1: ⟨7⟩. ⟨11⟩. ⟨12⟩	(⟨12⟩ is an atom Pr)
pc2: ⟨7⟩. ⟨11⟩. ⟨13⟩. ⟨14⟩	(⟨14⟩ is an atom Pr)
pc3: ⟨16⟩. ⟨17⟩. ⟨18⟩	(⟨18⟩ is an atom Pr)

where bc means Ib chain and pc means Pr chain. Here we have seven Ib chains and three Pr chains.

The paired input-output relations are:

$(bc1, bc2, bc4) \rightarrow pc1 \Rightarrow (bc3, bc6)$ or ([3],[5],[9])→⟨12⟩ ⇒ ([6],[15])

$bc5 \rightarrow pc2 \Rightarrow bc6$ or [10] → ⟨14⟩ ⇒ [15]

$(bc2, bc3, bc6) \rightarrow pc3 \Rightarrow bc7$ or ([5],[6],[15])→ ⟨18⟩ ⇒ [19]

This is the infobody model for the infobody structure in Figure 3.4.

The paired adjacency matrices are:

Table 3.3   Input Adjacency Matrix

	pc1: <12>	pc2: <14>	pc3: <18>	RSum	
bc1: [3]	1	0	0	1	
bc2: [5]	1	0	1	2	
bc3: [6]	0	0	1	1	
bc4: [9]	1	0	0	1	
bc5: [10]	0	1	0	1	
bc6: [15]	0	0	1	1	
bc7: [19]	0	0	0	0	Ending Ib

Table 3.4   Output Adjacency Matrix

	bc1: [3]	bc2: [5]	bc3: [6]	bc4: [9]	bc5: [10]	bc6: [15]	bc7: [19]
pc1: <12>	0	0	1	0	0	1	0
pc2: <14>	0	0	0	0	0	1	0
pc3: <18>	0	0	0	0	0	0	1
CSum	0	0	1	0	0	2	1
	Starting Ib	Starting Ib		Starting Ib	Starting Ib		

The IPO table for this infobody model is shown in Table 3.5.

Table 3.5   IPO Table

I	P	O
[3]	<12>	[6]
[5]	<12>	[15]
[9]	<12>	NULL
[10]	<14>	[15]
[5]	<18>	[19]
[6]	<18>	NULL
[15]	<18>	NULL

3.8   S Function

S Function is a simplified function from the *select* statement in SQL for databases and specifically applied to the IPO Table for infobody model path analysis. Below is the definition of the *S Function* denoted as $\mathscr{S}()$:

$$\mathscr{S}\left(Column, Rows\right) \text{ returns a set of values for}$$
the specified *column* and specified *rows*   (3.49)

where *column* is a column in the IPO table to be returned.

The valid values for the *column* are I, P, and O. *Rows* are determined by another *column* with one or more specified values (similar to the *where* clause in SQL).

For example, for the IPO table in Table 3.5,

$$\mathscr{S}(P, I = [5]) = \{\langle 12\rangle, \langle 18\rangle\}$$
$$\mathscr{S}(O, P = \langle 12\rangle) = \{[6], [15]\}$$
$$\mathscr{S}(O, P = \langle 18\rangle) = \{[19]\}$$

From this example we can see atom Ib [5] may have impact to atom Ib [6], [15] and [19].

3.9   Path Analysis

There are mainly two types of path analysis in the infobody model: forward path analysis and backward path analysis. Forward path analysis is often used for impact analysis and change analysis to find out the impact of a change in an infobody to other infobodies. Backward path analysis is often used for lineage analysis to find out all infobodies that would impact a given infobody.

3.9.1   Forward Path Analysis

Forward path analysis is starting from a specific atom Ib_0 and find out all Ibs forward that would be impacted by Ib_0.

We can use the IPO Table (Table 3.2) and S Function to implement the forward path analysis in the steps as follows:

Step 1: Find Prs that take Ib_0 as an input:

$$\mathscr{S}\left(P, I = Ib_0\right) = \left\{Pr_{11}, Pr_{12}, \cdots, Pr_{1n_1}\right\} = P_1 \qquad (3.50)$$

where n_1 is the number of Prs that take Ib_0 as an input.

Step 2: Find Ibs that are outputs from the Prs in P_1:

$$\mathscr{S}\left(O, P = P_1\right) = \left\{Ib_{11}^{(O)}, Ib_{12}^{(O)}, \cdots, Ib_{1m_1}^{(O)}\right\} = O_1 \qquad (3.51)$$

where m_1 is the number of Ibs that are outputs from the Prs in P_1.

Step 3: Find Prs that take Ibs in O_1 as inputs:

$$\mathscr{S}\left(P, I = O_1\right) = \left\{Pr_{21}, Pr_{22}, \cdots, Pr_{2n_2}\right\} = P_2 \qquad (3.52)$$

where n_2 is the number of Prs that take Ibs in O_1 as inputs.

Step 4: Find Ibs that are outputs from the Prs in P_2:

$$\mathscr{S}\left(O, P = P_2\right) = \left\{Ib_{21}^{(O)}, Ib_{22}^{(O)}, \cdots, Ib_{2m_2}^{(O)}\right\} = O_2 \qquad (3.53)$$

where m_2 is the number of Ibs that are outputs from the Prs in P_2.

In general, Step $2s - 1$: Find Prs that take Ibs in O_{s-1} as inputs:

$$\mathscr{S}\left(P, I = O_{s-1}\right) = \left\{Pr_{s1}, Pr_{s2}, \cdots, Pr_{sn_s}\right\} = P_s \qquad (3.54)$$

where n_s is the number of Prs that take Ibs in O_{s-1} as inputs.

Step $2s$: Find Ibs that are outputs from the Prs in P_s:

$$\mathscr{S}\left(O, P = P_s\right) = \left\{Ib_{s1}^{(O)}, Ib_{s2}^{(O)}, \cdots, Ib_{sm_s}^{(O)}\right\} = O_s \qquad (3.55)$$

where m_s is the number of Ibs that are outputs from the Prs in P_s.

Stop when P_s is empty and all Ibs in O_{s-1} are ending Ibs—recall (3.47).

The result of the forward path analysis (denoted as FW) is the union of all output sets:

$$FW = O_1 \cup O_2 \cup \cdots \cup O_s \qquad (3.56)$$

3.9.2 Backward Path Analysis

Backward path analysis is starting from a specific atom Ib_0 and find out all Ibs backward that would impact Ib_0.

The steps are similar to the steps for forward path analysis, but we need to go backward:

Step 1: Find Prs that generate Ib_0 as an output:

$$\mathscr{S}\left(P, O = Ib_0\right) = \left\{ Pr_{11}, Pr_{12}, \cdots, Pr_{1n_1} \right\} = P_1 \qquad (3.57)$$

where n_1 is the number of Prs that generate Ib_0 as an output.

Step 2: Find Ibs that are inputs to the Prs in P_1:

$$\mathscr{S}\left(I, P = P_1\right) = \left\{ Ib_{11}^{(I)}, Ib_{12}^{(I)}, \cdots, Ib_{1m_1}^{(I)} \right\} = I_1 \qquad (3.58)$$

where m_1 is the number of Ibs that are inputs to the Prs in P_1.

Step 3: Find Prs that generate Ibs in I_1 as outputs:

$$\mathscr{S}\left(P, O = I_1\right) = \left\{ Pr_{21}, Pr_{22}, \cdots, Pr_{2n_2} \right\} = P_2 \qquad (3.59)$$

where n_2 is the number of Prs that generate Ibs in I_1 as outputs.

Step 4: Find Ibs that are inputs to the Prs in P_2:

$$\mathscr{S}\left(I, P = P_2\right) = \left\{ Ib_{21}^{(I)}, Ib_{22}^{(I)}, \cdots, Ib_{2m_2}^{(I)} \right\} = I_2 \qquad (3.60)$$

where m_2 is the number of Ibs that are inputs to the Prs in P_2.

In general, Step $2s - 1$: Find Prs that generate Ibs in I_{s-1} as outputs:

$$\mathscr{S}\left(P, O = I_{s-1}\right) = \left\{ Pr_{s1}, Pr_{s2}, \cdots, Pr_{sn_s} \right\} = P_s \qquad (3.61)$$

where n_s is the number of Prs that generate Ibs in I_{s-1} as outputs.

Step 2s: Find Ibs that are inputs to the Prs in P_s:

$$\mathscr{S}\left(I, P = P_s\right) = \left\{ Ib_{s1}^{(I)}, Ib_{s2}^{(I)}, \cdots, Ib_{sm_s}^{(I)} \right\} = I_s \qquad (3.62)$$

where m_s is the number of Ibs that are inputs to the Prs in P_s.

Stop when P_s is empty and all Ibs in I_{s-1} are starting Ibs—recall (3.48).

The result of the backward path analysis (denoted as BW) is the union of all input sets:

$$BW = I_1 \cup I_2 \cup \cdots \cup I_s \qquad (3.63)$$

Forward path analysis and backward path analysis presented here are the primary algorithms and methodologies for any path analysis in an infobody model. Based on them, we may do a biward path analysis between two Ibs, and the result is simply $FW \cap BW$, the intersection of FW and BW. We may also do a similar path analysis for processor changes (e.g., business rule change) to examine the change impacts. Many specific path analysis algorithms can be developed by specifying more conditions for specific analytical purposes.

Now let's do the forward path analysis for the starting Ib [3] using the sample IPO in Table 3.5:

Step 1: $\mathscr{S}(P, I = [3]) = \{\langle 12 \rangle\} = P_1$

Step 2: $\mathscr{S}(O, P = \langle 12 \rangle) = \{[6], [15]\} = O_1$

Step 3: $\mathscr{S}(P, I = \{[6], [15]\}) = \{\langle 18 \rangle\} = P_2$

Step 4: $\mathscr{S}(O, P = \langle 18 \rangle) = \{[19]\} = O_2$

Step 5: $\mathscr{S}(P, I = [19]) = \{NULL\}$

Stop and $FW = O_1 \cup O_2 = \{[6], [15], [19]\}$ which are the impacted Ibs by [3].

Similarly, for ending Ib [19], the backward path analysis can be done as below:

Step 1: $\mathscr{S}(P, O = [19]) = \{\langle 18 \rangle\} = P_1$

Step 2: $\mathscr{S}(I, P = \langle 18 \rangle) = \{[5], [6], [15]\} = I_1$

Step 3: $\mathscr{S}(P, O = \{[5], [6], [15]\}) = \{\langle 12 \rangle, \langle 14 \rangle\} = P_2$

Step 4: $\mathscr{S}(I, P = \{\langle 12 \rangle, \langle 14 \rangle\}) = \{[3], [5], [9], [10]\} = I_2$

Step 5: $\mathscr{S}(P, O = \{[3], [5], [9], [10]\}) = \{NULL\}$

Stop and $BW = I_1 \cup I_2 = \{[3],[5],[6],[9],[10],[15]\}$ which are the lineage Ibs that impact Ib [19].

The biward result is $\{[6],[15],[19]\} \cap \{[3],[5],[6],[9],[10],[15]\} = \{[6],[15]\}$ which are the lineage Ibs to Ib [19] but impacted by Ib [3].

CHAPTER 4

CHAOS AND ENTROPY IN INFOBODY STRUCTURES

In Chapter 3, we presented a general infobody model in terms of graph theory which is a good tool for structural analysis for any infobody structures, and we presented some algorithms for path analysis in an infobody model. Path analysis does not include any numerical measure, but numerical measures are important for evaluation and optimization for an infobody structure. We may define a variety of measures in an infobody model, and some info-bodies themselves are numerical measures such as financial measures like sales, revenue, cost, and profit.

In this chapter, we are going to discuss a specific measure called entropy based on the concept of chaos in any infobody structures. We can use entropy to evaluate, improve, and optimize an infobody structure.

4.1 Chaos in Infobody Structures

We define *chaos* in an infobody structure as the *hardness to find the truth*. Then what is truth? In the infobody terminology, truth is a reality infobody which is a reality existence. But the reality existence may not last long, and not everyone can see, hear, or feel it for whatever reasons. Therefore, in some cases, it might be very hard to find the truth, especially when some people and organizations want to hide or even destroy the reality infobodies.

Let's take a look at some chaos cases:

- Different terms for the same thing

  In our daily life and business work, we often use different terms for the same thing. For example, a report developer gets two report requirements, one for "earning" and one for "margin," but in the database, the developer can only find "profit" data, then the developer needs to spend a lot of time talking to the business users to find the right people, and at the end of the day, the answer is all three terms mean the same thing.

- Different things with the same term

  On the other side, we also often use exactly the same term to mean different things. A typical example in our daily life is the same name for many different people. In business work, it often happens that a manager reads two reports and asks why the two reported values are different for the same measure. Then someone needs to spend a lot of time to find the two developers for the two reports, and then the two developers need to spend a lot of time to check and compare the results step-by-step, and finally, they may find the filters are different in the two reports.

- People may be scared to tell the truth

  If a person committed a crime, he might try to hide the truth or even destroy the pieces of evidence.

  If a criminal gang committed a crime, the crime leader might command the members not to tell the truth and destroy the pieces of evidence.

- Human brains are fuzzy

Human brains can remember a lot of things but often very fuzzy and may not last too long. So if one person is a witness for a crime and he cannot remember the exact time and what was happening and he can only say, "I cannot remember," "I am not sure," "Perhaps," etc., this would increase the hardness to find the truth.

- Human organs may have hardness to function well

    In a big meeting, people are very hard to catch what the speaker says. Even two people are talking very closely, they may still not be able to catch all words correctly from the other sides.

- Hard to find what you want

    Even now we have Google and many other search engines, sometimes, it is still very hard to find what you want exactly although the search engine can display a few million results in less than one second.

- Sometimes your computer is running very slow

    Everyone wants everything ASAP, but sometimes, your computer may run very slow to get a result.

4.2   Entropy

Entropy is the measure of chaos. As we defined before, chaos is the hardness to find truth, and so the first factor in measuring the hardness is the time obviously. The longer time to find the truth, the hardness is higher. But when we get an infobody, how can we tell it is true or not, or to what degree can we trust it? This is the concept of credibility. Also, it is understandable that the higher the credibility is, the hardness is lower. Another factor is the life time of the output infobody. Written text can last much longer time than oral language and easier to find the truth. So the definition of entropy should include these three factors: processing time to generate the output infobody, lifetime the output infobody can be lasting, and the credibility of the output infobody.

4.2.1 Basic Entropy

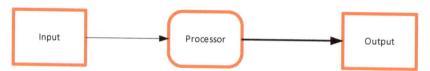

Figure 4.1   Single Infobody Structure

We define *basic entropy* in a single infobody structure shown in Figure 4.1 as below:

$$E^{(B)} = \frac{T}{L \cdot C} \qquad (4.1)$$

where $E^{(B)}$ is the basic entropy of the infobody structure, T is the processing time of the processor to generate the output infobody, L is the life time the output infobody can be lasting, and C is the *credibility* of the output infobody, which is defined as a percentage that the user can trust as the truth (will be discussed in more details in Section 4.3). In this formula, all numbers (T, L, and C) are positive or zero.

Time is a physical measure and is studied by a lot of scientists over a hundred years. In nowadays, we use it everywhere. Since T and L are both measured in time units, so the entropy has no physical unit.

As a single infobody structure in Figure 4.1, the atom output infobody is assumed at the value level such as a number in a column of a database table, a sentence in an article, a sentence in a speech, a picture, or a scene in a video.

Note, infobody, as a physical body, usually has a space volume such as a printed document or a file in a computer. In case we need to consider space volume, we can add the space volume S into the definition of entropy (4.1), and it would become:

$$E^{(B)} = \frac{T \cdot S}{L \cdot C} \qquad (4.2)$$

But not all infobodies take a space volume such as sound. In that case, the entropy E would be 0. Also, the space volume does not directly relate to the chaos—hardness to find the truth. Therefore, the basic entropy definition (4.1) does not include space volume S.

4.2.2 Normalized Entropy

The basic entropy definition (4.1) has a problem: $E^{(B)}$ will be infinitive ∞ when $C = 0$. To fix this issue, we define *normalized entropy* $E^{(N)}$ as below:

$$E^{(N)} = \frac{1}{e^{\left(\frac{1}{E^{(B)}}\right)}} = \frac{1}{e^{\left(\frac{L \cdot C}{T}\right)}} = e^{-\left(\frac{L \cdot C}{T}\right)} \qquad (4.3)$$

where e is the Euler's number.

The value of the normalized entropy $E^{(N)}$ is between 0 and 1 and

$$E^{(N)} = 1 \text{ when } C = 0 \qquad (4.4)$$
$$E^{(N)} \to 1 \text{ when } T \to \infty \qquad (4.5)$$
$$E^{(N)} \to 0 \text{ when } T \to 0 \qquad (4.6)$$

The basic entropy (4.1) and normalized entropy (4.3) are both defined for a single infobody structure shown in Figure 4.1

4.3 Credibility

In the definition of entropy, the hard part is the credibility C—how to define and calculate it.

First thing for calculating the credibility is that the definition of credibility must be based on numerical values, but not all infobodies are numerical values such as text, pictures, and videos. Fortunately, the credibility is trying to define the difference between the infobody value and the truth value. If the values are numerical, it is easy to define the difference as described below. If the values are not numerical such as text, pictures, and videos, we can still ask a simple question to get the answer "yes," denoted as number 1, or "no," denoted as number 0. For example, the name of person A is "Mike Smith," and the text "John Larson" is not the name of person A, so it would get a value of 0, and the text "Mike Smith" would get the value of 1 for person A's name. Also, name can be separated into first name and last name, and so the text "Mike Larson" would get the first name correct (1) and the last name wrong (0) for person A. Even for pictures and videos, we can still answer similar questions to get the value of 0 or 1.

Another basic rule is that the credibility C must be a positive value and between 0 and 1, so it is like a percentage. For example, $C = 0.2$ can give a sense that the infobody should not be trusted. If $C = 0.9$, then we can say that infobody can be trusted. $C = 0$ means cannot be trusted at all, and $C = 1$ means can be trusted absolutely. Furthermore, $C = 0.2$ and $C = 0$ are still with a small difference that $C = 0.2$ means the infobody might be trusted a little bit, and $C = 0$ means cannot be trusted at all. In fact, we would like to get some idea about the true value from the credibility. Say the infobody value is 10, and the credibility is 0.1, if the measure is "the greater, the better," then the true value would be 1. If the measure is "the less, the better," then the true value would be 100.

The point is how we can know the true value. In fact, we may use historical data to find out the true value so the credibility can be estimated. Then use the credibility to estimate the true value for the current situation.

To define the credibility, we set up the basic rules below:

Rule 1: Simple enough for easy understanding
Rule 2: Positive number or 0

Rule 3: Between 0 and 1
Rule 4: It should be a decreasing function of the distance
between the infobody value and the true value
Rule 5: Not too complicated for estimating the true value

Also, we need to understand a nature of a measure which is the willingness of the people to the measure. For example, any business wants the revenue the greater, the better and wants the cost the less, the better. Also, they want the profit the greater, the better. Because of this kind of willingness, people tend to lie or cheat to exaggerate or shrink the numbers. This is the basic reason that we need to estimate the credibility. In some specific cases, the measure may have a "best value" that people want the numbers the closer to this value, the better. Sometimes, the best value becomes a "best range" that people want the numbers within the range as much as possible.

To simplify writing, we will use some abbreviations for the willingness nature shown in Table 4.1:

Table 4.1   **Willingness Abbreviations**

Abbreviation	Willingness
GB	The greater, the better
LB	The less, the better
BV	Best value (the closer to the best value, the better)
BR	Best range (the closer to the best range, the better)

Now we are going to present a methodology for calculating the credibility as follows.

4.3.1   Basic credibility

For nonnegative values, we define the *basic credibility* as:

$$C^{(B)} = \frac{\min\left\{V^{(I)}, V^{(*)}\right\}}{\max\left\{V^{(I)}, V^{(*)}\right\}} \tag{4.7}$$

93

where $C^{(B)}$ is the basic credibility, $V^{(I)}$ is the numeric value of the infobody, and $V^{(*)}$ is the numeric value of the truth.

We call this operation (4.7) *min by max division* and simplify it using a new operator "//" as:

$$C^{(B)} = V^{(I)} \text{ // } V^{(*)} = V^{(*)} \text{ // } V^{(I)} \tag{4.8}$$

and we define

$$0 \text{ // } 0 = 1 \tag{4.9}$$

For example, if the true value is 10 and the infobody value is 100, then $C^{(B)} = 10/100 = 10\%$. If the true value is 10 and the infobody value is 1, then $C^{(B)} = 1/10 = 10\%$. They have the same credibility 10%, but the former one means exaggerating ten times, and the latter one means shrinking ten times.

Usually, a measure has a nature for "good" or "bad." Everyone wants the good measure—the greater, the better and wants the bad measure—the less, the better. So naturally, it is easy to tell the meaning of a credibility for exaggeration or shrink.

There is another case called "best value" for some measures. In this case, the measure is neither "the greater, the better" nor "the less, the better," but "the closer to a specific value, the better."

Note, all credibility calculations are based on the true value and true time (the time to find the truth), which means we can really calculate the credibilities only when the truth has been found. To this specific case, the credibility calculations seem meaningless, but it is still meaningful for the future. All calculated credibilities can become the useful estimates for the future similar cases, and we can estimate the true values based on the historical credibilities.

4.3.2　Cheating Coefficient

For easy calculation, we define another measure called *cheating coefficient* (denoted as γ) as below:

$$\gamma = V^{(I)} / V^{(*)} \tag{4.10}$$

and

$$0/0 = 1 \tag{4.11}$$

The relationship between the credibility and the cheating coefficient is shown below:

$$C^{(B)} = \gamma \text{ if } V^{(I)} \leq V^{(*)} \text{ for the less the better case} \tag{4.12}$$

$$C^{(B)} = \frac{1}{\gamma} \text{ if } V^{(I)} > V^{(*)} \text{ for the greater the better case} \tag{4.13}$$

4.3.3　Other Cases

The basic credibility and cheating coefficient can be applied only to the nonnegative numbers. But in some cases, we may have to deal with negative numbers. For example, in business accounting, Profit = Revenue – Cost, and we may get negative numbers for Profit when Revenue < Cost.

We will denote the three possible number cases as below:

Case (+, +): Both infobody value and true value are positive.
Case (-, -): Both infobody value and true values are negative.
Case (+, -): One (infobody or true) value is positive, and the other is negative.

4.3.4 Case (-, -)

We can simply apply the basic credibility $C^{(B)}$ (4.7) and (4.8) to this case with a little change:

$$C^{(B)} = \frac{\min\left\{\left|V^{(I)}\right|,\left|V^{(*)}\right|\right\}}{\max\left\{\left|V^{(I)}\right|,\left|V^{(*)}\right|\right\}} \tag{4.14}$$

$$C^{(B)} = \left|V^{(I)}\right| // \left|V^{(*)}\right| = \left|V^{(*)}\right| // \left|V^{(I)}\right| \tag{4.15}$$

Here the only change is to use absolute values to make them all positive.

4.3.5 Case (+, -): Displacement Transformation

This case is more complicated. Let us take an example. Suppose the infobody value $V^{(I)}$ is 3, and the true value $V^{(*)}$ is -3. If we use formula (4.7), we will get $C^{(B)} = -3/3 = -1$, which is conflicting to the definition of credibility. Even if we use formula (4.14), we will get $C^{(B)} = 3/3 = 1$, which is obviously wrong because $V^{(I)} - V^{(*)} = 6$, but we got $C^{(B)} = 1 = 100\%$.

So to deal with the (+, -) case, we will need some transformations to make the numbers both positive or both negative then apply the basic formula (4.7) or (4.14). Let us use the example below to show our method and then summarize it into theoretical formulas.

Example: Profit infobody value $V^{(I)} = 0.2$ million, true value $V^{(*)} = -0.3$ million and the profit measure has a GB nature. Since the difference between 0.2 and -0.3 is $0.2 - (-0.3) = 0.5$, we can find a negative number -0.8 with the same difference 0.5 from the true value -0.3 by the following transformation:

$$-0.3 - 0.5 = -0.8 \tag{4.16}$$

Then apply formula (4.14), we can get

$$C^{(D)} = \frac{\min\{|-0.8|\,,\,|-0.3|\}}{\max\{|-0.8|\,,\,|-0.3|\}} = \frac{0.3}{0.8} = 0.375 \qquad (4.17)$$

where $C^{(D)}$ is called *displaced credibility.* The transformation (4.16) is called *displacement transformation,* as demonstrated in Figure 4.2.

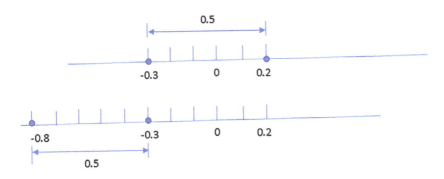

Figure 4.2   Displacement Transformation

Based on this example, we can generalize the method to the following formulas:

Suppose infobody value $V^{(I)} > 0$ and the true value $V^{(*)} < 0$ then the displacement transformation is:

$$V^{(D)} = V^{(*)} - \left(V^{(I)} - V^{(*)}\right) = 2V^{(*)} - V^{(I)} \qquad (4.18)$$

where $V^{(D)}$ is called *displaced value.*

If $V^{(I)} < 0$ and $V^{(*)} > 0$ then

$$V^{(D)} = V^{(*)} + \left(V^{(*)} - V^{(I)}\right) = 2V^{(*)} - V^{(I)} \qquad (4.19)$$

From (4.18) and (4.19), we can see the formulas are the same. Then (4.14) can give the displaced credibility $C^{(D)}$.

4.3.6   Time Gradient and Credibility Gradient

The credibility values may change along with the time (info-body processing time). For example, a criminal says "no" for his offense ($C_0 = 0$) in a trial. Ten days later, in another trial, he says "yes" for some of his offense (say 20 percent and so $C_1 = 0.2$). Another ten days later, in another trial, he says "yes" for all his offense (100 percent and so $C^{(*)} = 1$). This example can be demonstrated in Figure 4.3.

Figure 4.3   Example of Time Gradient

We can define a new measure called *time gradient* to check the changes:

$$Tg = \frac{\Delta T}{\Delta C} = \frac{T_2 - T_1}{C_2 - C_1} \tag{4.20}$$

where T_i is the processing time of infobody i ($i = 1, 2$) with credibility C_i.

From formula (4.20), we can calculate the time gradient for the points in the example:

$$Tg_1 = \frac{10 - 0}{0.2 - 0} = 50$$

$$Tg_2 = \frac{20 - 10}{1 - 0.2} = 12.5$$

$$Tg^{(*)} = \frac{20-0}{1-0} = 20$$

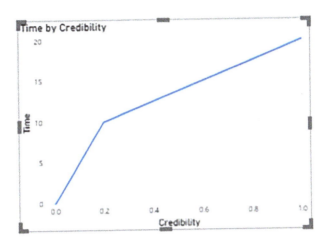

Figure 4.4   Time Gradient Chart

These points can be drawn in a chart shown in Figure 4.4. From the chart, we can see the first part of the line is pretty steep ($Tg_1 = 50$). The second part is much flatter ($Tg_2 = 12.5$).

Time gradient can be used to analyze the cheating patterns of the credibility of a person or organization.

Similarly, we can define credibility gradient as:

$$Cg = \frac{\Delta C}{\Delta T} = \frac{C_2 - C_1}{T_2 - T_1} \tag{4.21}$$

which can be used to analyze the credibility changes per unit of processing time.

4.3.7 Equal Entropy Rule and Adjusted Credibility

We present an equal entropy rule here based on the definitions of chaos and entropy. Chaos is the hardness to find the truth, and the entropy is the numerical measure of the chaos.

It is easy to understand that the simplest measure for entropy is the time to find the truth if the truth has been found. But in most cases, the truth might not have been found, and we want to get some idea about the credibility and the entropy based on the historical data. Theoretically, for the same case, the entropy should be equal at any time with any infobody generated by the main processor, such as the confessions from the criminal in a crime case.

But from the entropy formula (4.1):

$$E^{(B)} = \frac{T}{L \cdot C} \tag{4.22}$$

and the credibility formula (4.7):

$$C^{(B)} = \frac{\min\{V^{(I)}, V^{(*)}\}}{\max\{V^{(I)}, V^{(*)}\}} \tag{4.23}$$

we may not get the same entropy value at all points in time. For this reason, we present the *equal entropy rule* as follows: The entropy is the same at any point of time with the infobody generated by the main processor in an infobody structure.

Based on the equal entropy rule, we will need to modify the entropy formula (4.22) as follows:

$$E^{(A)} = \frac{T}{L \cdot (\alpha C + \beta)} \tag{4.24}$$

where α and β are two constants for the entropy adjustment called *entropy constants,* and $E^{(A)}$ is called the *adjusted entropy* and

$$C^{(A)} = (\alpha C + \beta) \qquad (4.25)$$

is called *adjusted credibility*.

Note, $E^{(A)}$ (4.24) is applied to all-time points except for the end time (truth found).

To calculate or estimate the entropy constants, we need to have at least two nonending points: the start time T_1 (the first info-body generated by the main processor) and the second time T_2 before the truth found end point, so we can have two equations:

$$E_1^{(A)} = \frac{T_1}{L(\alpha C_1 + \beta)} = E^{(*)} = \frac{T^{(*)}}{LC^{(*)}} = \frac{T^{(*)}}{L \cdot 1} = \frac{T^{(*)}}{L} \qquad (4.26)$$

$$E_2^{(A)} = \frac{T_2}{L(\alpha C_2 + \beta)} = E^{(*)} = \frac{T^{(*)}}{LC^{(*)}} = \frac{T^{(*)}}{L \cdot 1} = \frac{T^{(*)}}{L} \qquad (4.27)$$

where * indicates the end time (the truth is found).

From (4.26) and (4.27), we can have a simple equation system:

$$\begin{cases} \alpha C_1 + \beta = \dfrac{T_1}{T^{(*)}} \\[2mm] \alpha C_2 + \beta = \dfrac{T_2}{T^{(*)}} \end{cases} \qquad (4.28)$$

Solve this equation system, and we can get the solution for α and β:

$$\alpha = \frac{T_2 - T_1}{T^{(*)}(C_2 - C_1)} \qquad (4.29)$$

$$\beta = \frac{T_1 C_2 - T_2 C_1}{T^{(*)}(C_2 - C_1)} \qquad (4.30)$$

If $C_1 = 0$ (e.g., the criminal said no to everything) then

$$\alpha C_1 + \beta = \beta = \frac{T_1}{T^{(*)}} \tag{4.31}$$

is the adjusted credibility.

Now suppose we have n nonending points, then we can have a similar equation system:

$$\begin{cases} \alpha C_1 + \beta = \dfrac{T_1}{T^{(*)}} \\[2mm] \alpha C_2 + \beta = \dfrac{T_2}{T^{(*)}} \\[2mm] \vdots \\[2mm] \alpha C_n + \beta = \dfrac{T_n}{T^{(*)}} \end{cases} \tag{4.32}$$

This is a typical regression problem, and we can use the least square method to get the estimates:

$$\alpha = \frac{\sum_{i=1}^{n}\left(C_i - \bar{C}\right)\left(t_i - \bar{t}\right)}{\sum_{i=1}^{n}\left(C_i - \bar{C}\right)^2} \tag{4.33}$$

$$\beta = \bar{t} - \alpha\bar{C} \tag{4.34}$$

$$\bar{C} = \frac{1}{n}\sum_{i=1}^{n} C_i \tag{4.35}$$

$$\bar{t} = \frac{1}{n}\sum_{i=1}^{n} t_i \tag{4.36}$$

$$t_i = \frac{T_i}{T^{(*)}} \quad (i = 1, 2, \ldots, n) \qquad (4.37)$$

4.3.8 Probability for Random Credibility

For each individual value of an atom infobody, the credibility C (either basic or adjusted) is a constant. For a set of atom info-bodies contained in a container infobody, the credibility becomes a variable defined on the set of all possible values of the contained atom infobodies. Furthermore, this variable is a random variable with a probability distribution for the credibility values of the atom infobodies.

A typical example is a column in a database table that con-tains many values in all rows, and each value has a credibility. Suppose this column contains eleven distinct credibilities with corresponding frequencies shown in Table 4.2:

Table 4.2   Sample Credibilities of the Values in a Database Table Column

Value	Credibility	Frequency
0	0	1
16	0.1	3
32	0.2	5
48	0.3	9
64	0.4	14
80	0.5	17
96	0.6	9
112	0.7	4
128	0.8	3
144	0.9	2
160	1	1

The frequency can be shown in a histogram as in Figure 4.5.

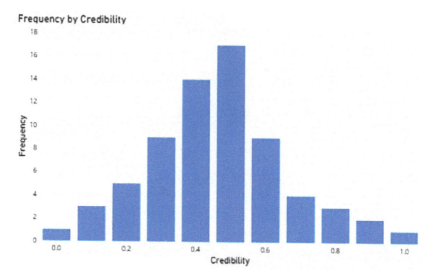

Figure 4.5   Histogram of Credibilities

Figure 4.5 suggests a probability distribution for the random variable credibility. Assume the probability density function is $p(x)$ for the credibility random variable C, then we can calculate the mathematical expectation (MEx) and variance (Var):

$$MEx(C) = \int_0^1 x \cdot p(x)dx \qquad (4.38)$$

$$Var(C) = \int_0^1 (x - MEx(C))^2 \cdot p(x)dx \qquad (4.39)$$

In statistics for sampled data, (4.38) and (4.39) become:

$$MEx(C) = \sum_{i=1}^n x_i \cdot p_i \qquad (4.40)$$

$$Var(C) = \sum_{i=1}^n (x_i - MEx(C))^2 \cdot p_i \qquad (4.41)$$

where x_i is the i-th sample value of the credibility C; p_i is the probability of x_i .

For the example data listed in Table 4.2, we can get:

$$MEx(C) = 0.463235$$

$$Var(C) = 0.039384$$

The detailed calculations are listed in Table 4.3.

Table 4.3   Calculations for MEx and Var

Value	Credibility	Frequency	Probability	MEx	Var
0	0	1	1.47%	0	0.003156
16	0.1	3	4.41%	0.004412	0.005821
32	0.2	5	7.35%	0.014706	0.005095
48	0.3	9	13.24%	0.039706	0.003527
64	0.4	14	20.59%	0.082353	0.000823
80	0.5	17	25.00%	0.125	0.000338
96	0.6	9	13.24%	0.079412	0.002476
112	0.7	4	5.88%	0.041176	0.003298
128	0.8	3	4.41%	0.035294	0.005003
144	0.9	2	2.94%	0.026471	0.005611
160	1	1	1.47%	0.014706	0.004237
	Sum	68		**0.463235**	**0.039384**

Note, for even distribution $p_i = \dfrac{1}{n}$, then (4.40) and (4.41) become the regular average and variance.

4.4   Thinking Structure

Most infobodies are generated by human beings. Most human beings are honest for most events. But for some specific events more directly related to themselves, they may not be absolutely honest. They may not be willing to tell the truth for some reason which means they may cheat intentionally. Even if they want to tell the truth, they may not catch the truth for some physical difficulties. For example, a person talks to another. The second person may not catch the words completely and correctly because the distance may be too far, and the wind may be too strong.

The infobody structure in a human being's brain for a certain event, from catching the reality infobodies to generating one or more new infobodies, such as generating new images in the brain or saying some words or writing some text or taking pictures or videos, is called a *thinking structure*.

Figure 4.6 is an infobody chart describing a general thinking structure.

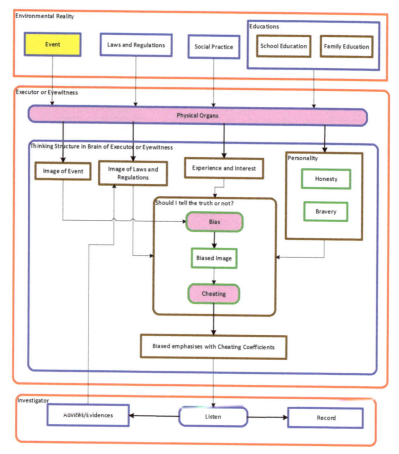

**Figure 4.6   Thinking Structure in the
Brain of Executor or Eyewitness**

In Figure 4.6, we highlighted three processors: ⟨Organs⟩, ⟨Bias⟩ and ⟨Cheating⟩, which we will discuss in more detail here.

4.4.1 Physical Organs—Physical Credibility

Physical organs (eyes, ears, noses, etc.) are the first set of infobody processors that translate the reality infobodies—[Event] into the images in the brain of an executor or eyewitness. But those images in the brain can never reproduce the reality event 100 percent completely and correctly. This is the physical distortion, and we want to keep the fidelity as high as possible.

We can use a multidimensional model to describe the event in reality and use the basic credibility (4.7) to measure the fidelity. An event usually can be described in a number of dimensions such as time, location, number of people (for a lot of people), or names of the executors and eyewitnesses (for a single person or a few people). A big event can be divided into a series of sub-events by time for what was happening.

As an executor or eyewitness, he or she obtained an image about the reality event, but the image can never contain all details about the event. For example, suppose the event is a public event, and all TV channels used many video cameras to keep the records of the event and suppose we can review all scenes of the event. Then we can calculate the basic credibility for each dimension measure using the basic credibility formula (4.7):

$$C_j^{(Ph)} = \frac{\min\left\{V_j^{(Ph)}, V_j^{(*)}\right\}}{\max\left\{V_j^{(Ph)}, V_j^{(*)}\right\}} \qquad (4.42)$$

where $V_j^{(Ph)}$ is the value of the j-th dimension measure caught by the physical organs. We can use formula (4.8) to simplify it as

$$C_j^{(Ph)} = V_j^{(Ph)} \,//\, V_j^{(*)} = V_j^{(*)} \,//\, V_j^{(Ph)} \qquad (4.43)$$

Then the credibility of [Image of Event] infobody, denoted as $C^{(Ph)}$, can be defined as the average of all basic credibilities:

$$C^{(Ph)} = \frac{1}{n}\Sigma_{j=1}^{n}\, C_j^{(Ph)} \tag{4.44}$$

Usually, the credibility of [Image of Event] infobody is non-intentional and purely caused by the physical environment and physical performances of the organs, and so we call it *physical credibility*.

The infobody structure $[\text{Event}] \rightarrow \text{Organs} \Rightarrow [\text{Image of Event}]$ is called *physical thinking structure*.

4.4.2 Bias

In the thinking structure of the executor or eyewitness, he or she needs to think the question ⟨Should I tell the truth or not?⟩, which is a processor to process the image of the event. If he or she is honest and brave, he or she can simply tell the truth from the infobody [Image of Event]. Sometimes, for whatever reason, he or she may not be willing to tell the truth and want to lie. Usually, the lying process contains two main aspects: bias and cheating.

Bias in thinking structure is to emphasize focus on some aspects and contempt or ignore other aspects. Suppose we separate the time period into n smaller segments based on the true event process and denote the *true segmentation* as

$$S_1^{(*)}, S_2^{(*)}, \cdots, S_n^{(*)} \tag{4.45}$$

and

$$S^{(*)} = \Sigma_{j=1}^{n} S_j^{(*)} \tag{4.46}$$

is the total time of the true event process. Then the percentages

$$W_j^{(*)} = \frac{S_j^{(*)}}{S^{(*)}} \; j = 1, 2, \cdots, n \qquad (4.47)$$

are called *true weighting* and

$$\sum_{j=1}^{n} W_j^{(*)} = 1 \qquad (4.48)$$

is the true weight of the true segment j in the whole event process.
　　Now suppose this eyewitness wants to emphasize the focus on some segments and contempt or ignore other segments by creating another set of weights, called *biased weighting*:

$$W_1^{(Bi)}, W_2^{(Bi)}, \cdots, W_n^{(Bi)} \qquad (4.49)$$

then

$$C_j^{(Bi)} = W_j^{(Bi)} / / W_j^{(*)} \qquad (4.50)$$

is called *biased credibility of segment j*, where

$$\sum_{j=1}^{n} W_j^{(Bi)} = 1 \qquad (4.51)$$

and

$$C^{(Bi)} = \sum_{j=1}^{n} C_j^{(Bi)} W_j^{(*)} \qquad (4.52)$$

is called the *biased credibility* of the whole event.

4.4.3 Cheating

With the infobody [Biased Image] in Figure 4.6, the executor or eyewitness may even want to change the measure values intentionally based on the physical organ values. Similar to the basic credibility, we can define the *cheating credibility* $C_j^{(Ch)}$ as:

$$C_j^{(Ch)} = V_j^{(Ch)} /\!/ V_j^{(Ph)} \qquad (4.53)$$

Note, the cheating credibility is based on the physical organ value $V_j^{(Ph)}$ for j-th dimension measure, and average cheating credibility for all dimension measures are:

$$C^{(Ch)} = \frac{1}{n}\sum_{j=1}^{n} C_j^{(Ch)} \qquad (4.54)$$

For the overall thinking structure, the *thinking credibility* $C^{(Th)}$ is defined as:

$$C^{(Th)} = C^{(Ph)} \cdot C^{(Bi)} \cdot C^{(Ch)} \qquad (4.55)$$

4.5 Credibility Transfer and Overall Entropy of an Infobody Structure

In an infobody structure, not all processors get the input from the reality infobodies. Most infobodies in an infobody structure are translated infobodies. A translated infobody has a credibility that may not be one. Suppose a processor adds two numbers N_1 and N_2 with credibilities C_1 and C_2, then what is the credibility for the sum $N_1 + N_2$? This is the topic of *credibility transfer*.

Let's start with the simplest operation—addition—using a simple example. Suppose $N_1 = 20$ with credibility $C_1 = 0.4$ and $N_2 = 30$ with credibility $C_2 = 0.7$, then what is the credibility for the sum 50? To solve this problem, we need to identify the willingness of the measure (see Table 4.1 Willingness Abbreviations).

Assume the willingness of this measure is GB (the greater, the better) then we can get the true values:

$$20 \times 0.4 = 8 \tag{4.56}$$
$$30 \times 0.7 = 21 \tag{4.57}$$

So the sum of the true values is

$$8 + 21 = 29 \tag{4.58}$$

and the credibility of the sum is

$$29 / 50 = 0.58 \tag{4.59}$$

From (4.56) – (4.59), we can derive some steps for a general transfer function result $r = f\left(V_1, V_2, \cdots, V_n\right)$ with credibility C_i for value V_i ($i = 1, 2, \cdots, n$) as follows:

Step 1: Calculate the true values $V_i^{(*)}$ from V_i and C_i ($i = 1, 2, \cdots, n$) based on the willingness.

$$V_i^{(*)} = V_i / \times C \tag{4.60}$$

where $/\times$ means either $/$ or $\times$ based on the willingness of the measure.

Step 2: Apply the transfer function f to the true values to get the true result $r^{(*)}$.

$$r^{(*)} = f\left(V_1^{(*)}, V_2^{(*)}, \cdots, V_n^{(*)}\right) \tag{4.61}$$

Step 3: Calculate the credibility for the result:

$$C^{(r)} = r / / r^{(*)} \tag{4.62}$$

Note, the result r and the true result $r^{(*)}$ may get negative values, and the credibility calculation should follow the rules described in Section 4.3.4 and Section 4.3.5.

We can denote the credibility transfer steps from (4.60) – (4.62) as a single formula:

$$C^{(r)} = Tr\left(C_1, C_2, \cdots, C_n\right) \qquad (4.63)$$

In a general infobody structure with human beings and the computers (or other devices), the thinking structure should be applied to the part of human beings, and the credibility transfer should be applied to the computer (or other devices) parts. This way, we can get the credibility for each final output infobody.

For a computer system, the transfer function $f()$ can be regarded as the entire infobody structure, which means run all for present values and true values to get final output for present and true output infobodies then calculate credibility for each output. This means no need to calculate the credibilities for every single intermediate result.

The overall entropy E of the entire infobody structure can be calculated as:

$$E = \frac{T}{L \cdot C} \qquad (4.64)$$

where T is the entire time to generate all final output infobodies, L is the lifetime of all final output infobodies, and C is the average credibility of all final output infobodies.

4.6 Infobody Structure Optimization

Entropy provides an index for any infobody structure, and we always have a willingness to minimize it. This becomes another important topic—*infobody structure optimization*.

There are three major factors in any optimization problem:

- *Decision variables.* The variables that we have control over to make changes
- *Objective function.* A function of decision variables that we want to optimize (minimize or maximize)
- *Constraints.* A set of functions of decision variables that we need to subject to

In our infobody structure optimization problem, the decision variable is any modification in the structure. Recall in Section 3.6, any infobody structure can be described as an infobody model ($\mathcal{C}$, $\mathcal{I} \sim \mathcal{O}$) with three parts: containing graph $\mathcal{C}$, paired input-output graphs $\mathcal{I}$ and $\mathcal{O}$. The modification M can be any addition, deletion, and change in these three parts. For example, technical progress to reduce the processing time T, technical progress to increase the lifetime L of infobody, education or lawsuit to increase the credibility, etc.

The objective function in our infobody structure optimization is usually to minimize the overall entropy (4.64).

The constraints in the optimization include two sets:

- *Content constraints.* The content definitions of the final output infobodies should not be changed. For example, "total sales" is the definition of an output infobody. The value may be changed by increasing the credibility, the physical body may be changed from a sound to a number on a computer screen, but the definition "total sales" can never be changed.
- *Financial constraints.* Any modification may cost extra money, so the total costs need to be subjected to the budget.

Now we can describe our infobody structure optimization model as follows:

$$\text{Min } E(M) = \frac{T(M)}{L(M) \cdot C(M)} \tag{4.65}$$

s.t.

$$S(M) \leq S^* \tag{4.66}$$

$$M \in (\mathscr{C}, \mathscr{I} \sim \mathscr{O}) \tag{4.67}$$

where M is the set of the modifications in the infobody structure ($\mathscr{C}\mathscr{I} \sim \mathscr{O}$), $T(M)$ is the total processing time after modifications M, $L(M)$ is the total lifetime of all final output infobodies after modifications M, and $C(M)$ is the average credibility of all final output infobodies. Formula (4.66) means the business constraints and financial constraints. Formula (4.67) means the modifications M is in the infobody structure ($\mathscr{C}\mathscr{I} \sim \mathscr{O}$) without changing the definitions of any final output infobodies.

Here we present an example to demonstrate the infobody structure optimization.

Example: Power BI Reporting

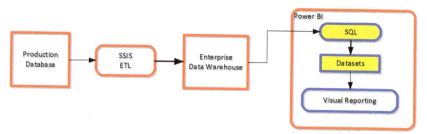

Figure 4.7   Power BI Reporting without SSAS Tabular Model

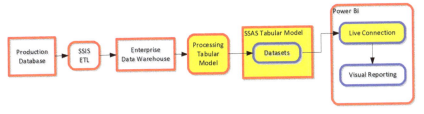

Figure 4.8   Power BI Reporting with SSAS Tabular Model

Power BI is a reporting tool from Microsoft for interactive reporting. The reporting teams in most companies develop Power BI reports and dashboards in the way shown in Figure 4.7, which means the report developer uses a SQL query within Power BI to import data from the EDW (enterprise data warehouse) to the Power BI directly and then creates reports and dashboards based on the imported datasets. The best practice is the way shown in Figure 4.8, which means the developer created an SSAS tabular model based on the EDW and then use a live connection in Power BI to connect to the tabular model and create reports based on the live connection.

Table 4.4 shows the performance for 162 reports. There are 10 reports each needs 30 seconds to show up for SQL reporting while the same 10 reports each only needs 3 seconds to show up for SSAS reporting. Note, SSAS needs 5 minutes (300 seconds) extra time to process (usually in the night nonworking hours). Other numbers have similar meanings. Notice in total, SQL reporting needs 186 minutes while SSAS reporting only needs 78 minutes, and no extra cost is needed because SSAS is included in the SQL Server.

Table 4.4   Power BI Reporting Performance (in Second)

	Number of Reports	Use SQL	Total SQL Reporting Time	Use SSAS	Total SSAS Reporting Time
	10	30	300	3	90
	24	35	840	2	70
	14	40	560	4	160

Table 4.4   (Continued)

	18	50	900	6	300
	12	60	720	4	240
	8	65	520	5	325
	30	80	2400	7	560
	11	95	1045	7	665
	15	100	1500	8	800
	20	120	2400	10	1200
Sum	162		11185		4410
SSAS Processing Time:				300	4710
Total Minutes			186.42		78.5

This example shows how to optimize an infobody structure by adding a new tool that is much more efficient to improve the performance (reduce the entropy).

REFERENCES

Clausius, R. 1867. *The Mechanical Theory of Heat—with Its Applications to the Steam Engine and to Physical Properties of Bodies*. London: John van Voorst.

Roberts, Fred S. 1976. *Discrete Mathematical Models with Applications to Social, Biological, and Environmental Problems*. Prentice-Hall.

Shannon, C. E. 1948. *A Mathematical Theory of Communication*. Bell System Technical Journal, 27, pp. 379–423 and 623–656.

ABOUT THE AUTHOR

YUHU CHE RECEIVED his PhD (1992) in geography with a focus on economic analysis for energy and environmental studies from Boston University, Boston, Massachusetts, USA. He has been working in various industries in USA with a focus on business intelligence for over twenty years. He has been thinking about the infobody concepts and topics over the last thirty years in his spare time and created the infobody theory and infobody model summarized in this book.

Yuhu Che would like to discuss the infobody topics with anyone who is interested in it, such as university professors and students, managers and employees in any business industries and government agencies. His dedicated email address for this topic is yuhuinfobody@gmail.com.

www.ingramcontent.com/pod-product-compliance
Lightning Source LLC
Chambersburg PA
CBHW041634050326
40689CB00024B/4960